PRAISE FOR THE KOREAN EDITION OF THIS BOOK

SELECTED AS "YOUNG ADULT BOOK OF THE YEAR" BY THE KOREAN PUBLISHERS ASSOCIATION

SELECTED AS A "RECOMMENDED BOOK" BY THE SCHOOL LIBRARY JOURNAL

"Yeong-dae's story blends reportage and children's fiction, giving readers a fresh understanding of life in North Korea and the history of North and South Korea. The well-crafted plot and the breathless narrative flow will engage young readers, too."

- School Library Journal

"A realistic description of how an ordinary boy becomes a *kkotjebi* and risks his life to cross the Tumen River into China."

-Kids' Chosun Ilbo

"*Across the Tumen* is a historical children's novel that vividly represents the difficult lives of North Korean children. Young readers may find themselves hoping that North Korean children can enjoy the same freedom as their counterparts in the South and that North and South Korea will be reunited before long. This is the powerful message that this children's story hopes to communicate to readers."

-Kids' Hankook Ilbo

D0018903

"The novel follows the tumultuous story of Yeong-dae and describes the horrors that he experiences at a young age. . . In various places in the book, one is struck by the power of love to remain strong amid a famine."

-Baek Na-ri, *Yonhap News*

"An accurate depiction of the human rights situation for North Korean children—describing how a North Korean boy becomes a *kkotjebi*, is thrown in prison, and eventually gains his freedom."

-Gi Su-jeong, *Aju News*

"When writing *Across the Tumen*, Moon gathered information by reading accounts written by North Korean defectors and meeting with North Korean writers. This allowed her to write a novel that could easily be a true story."

-Kim Ji-eun, *Ulsan Daily*

"Reading *Across the Tumen*, you can imagine the tragic lives faced by those who had the misfortune of being born in North Korea. . . As you follow Yeong-dae through this book, you will find yourself thinking long and hard about the food, clothing, and shelter that we take for granted. . . Moon is one of those rare writers who deal with such weighty topics."

-yunizini, Kyobo Books reviewer

ACROSS
THE TUMEN

Across the Tumen

This is a work of fiction. Names, characters, places, and incidents are either the product of the author's imagination or used fictitiously, and any resemblance to actual persons, living or dead, business establishments, events, or locales is entirely coincidental.

Published in the United States of America by Seoul Selection USA, Inc.
4199 Campus Dr., Suite 550
Irvine, CA 92612, USA
Tel: 949-509-6584
Fax: 949-509-6599
E-mail: publisher@seoulselection.com
Website: www.seoulselection.com

ISBN: 978-1-62412-009-1
Library of Congress Control Number: 2013956939

Printed in the Republic of Korea

ACROSS THE TUMEN

A North Korean *Kkotjebi* Boy's Quest

Moon Young-sook

Wipe Away the Tears of the Children

When I started reading this book, I found myself amazed that the author seemed to understand North Korean society even better than me—and I used to live there! I was sucked into the story, and it felt less like reading a novel and more like reliving my childhood and escape from North Korea. Around 25,000 North Koreans have defected to the South as of 2013, and it seemed like the heartbreaking tale of each defector was distilled into this story.

My job is spreading news of the human rights crisis in North Korea to the outside world, so I'm always looking for a better way to raise awareness in South Korea of the horrible reality of life in the North. I've tried a variety of methods, organized campaigns, seminars, and exhibitions for the general public, and met people from all walks of life to convince them of the importance of this issue. To my disappointment, South Koreans have not been as interested as I had expected.

Surprisingly, the plight of North Korean defectors is receiving more attention outside of South Korea than inside. On March 22, 2013, the United Nations Human Rights Council set up a commission of inquiry into human rights in the North. I was among those who testified before the commission about the state of human rights in the Stalinist country. More countries are taking interest in the North Korean issue and urging change. North Korea is no longer South Korea's problem but an issue that the world and all of humankind must work to resolve.

It was around this time that I read *Across the Tumen*, and it gave me a new perspective. Drawing on the power of literature, the book communicates with the masses in a way that is easy to understand. As readers join the main character Yeong-dae on his challenging journey, the plight of defectors will be driven home in a new way. It will no longer just be someone else's business. Whether young or old, everyone must be aware of this issue.

Even today, there are young North Koreans like Yeong-dae who are still suffering from the things described in the book. No one chooses to be born in North Korea, and no one there is content with the daily struggle to survive. Lording over the common people are the privileged classes, who deprive the former of freedom, rule the country through fear, and obsess over securing a life of wealth and luxury for them and their children. At the very bottom of the North's societal ladder are young *kkotjebi* like Yeong-dae, who clutch their empty bellies and battle each day with the fear of death.

Kim Young-il

Executive Director of PSCORE
(People for Successful Corean Reunification)
Jan 2014

Hope for the *Kkotjebi*

In spring 2011, I went on a week-long trip to the Yalu River with members of the Unification Literature Forum. Joining me were other writers longing for Korean reunification, people who wanted to see and feel North Korea up close. The North is South Korea's other half, but we cannot go there even if we want to.

As our bus rode along the Yalu from Dandong, China—just across from the North Korean city of Sinuiju—to Changchun, China, everything in North Korea we could see across the river was completely gray. No smoke had been seen coming out of Sinuiju factories for several years, we were told. The hills had been stripped of trees from top to bottom, and the slopes were planted with makeshift corn fields. This showed us at a glance how bad the food shortage was in the North.

During the mid-1990s, North Korea went through a severe famine that was called the "Arduous March." When the Soviet Union collapsed and former Soviet republics declared independence, the North was isolated. Drought led to famine, and soon it was hard for North Koreans to keep food on the table each day. People began to starve to death, and children with nowhere to go became *kkotjebi*—young beggars.

Throughout our trip, our Joseonjok (Korean-Chinese) guide described the horrors suffered by the people of North Korea during the Arduous March. We were told that countless people gathered at the banks of the Yalu, which separates North Korea from China, hoping that Joseonjok would help them. They waited there until they collapsed from exhaustion and died. Hearing this broke my heart.

About twenty years have passed since this tumultuous period, but sadly, the food situation in North Korea hasn't gotten much better. To help me flesh out Yeong-dae, the main character of this book, I read the memoirs of North Korean defectors and also had many conversations with North Korean writers who had fled to the South. Nearly all of the situations that appear here are based on real-life stories.

I wrote this book because I couldn't just stand by and watch as the young people who are supposed to lead North Korea into the future wander the streets and beg for food as *kkotjebi*. All children should have a happy childhood and be able to go to school at the right time no matter what. And yet, at this very moment, starving children in North Korea are forced to live on the streets. I hope that they can soon dream of a brighter future in a more stable country.

Moon Young-sook

Jan 2014

Contents

The Border

The sky above was as clear as a pane of glass, so clear that you could crack it just by touching it with a needle. There wasn't a single scrap of cloud that Yeong-dae could hide behind.

His heart had been pounding since the sun started falling toward the hills in the west. His friend Nam-sik swallowed nervously.

"Our fate will be settled tonight. After the night guards start their watch and finish their first patrol, that's when we cross. Since it's after midnight, the guards will take a short nap after their patrol is over," Nam-sik said.

"Fine, but what happens if we get caught?"

Nam-sik slugged Yeong-dae on the shoulder. "Do you want

to jinx us? If we're caught, we'll just say we were going to China to forage."

When people talked about "foraging," they meant leaving their town and going elsewhere to find food.

Yeong-dae shut his mouth and nodded. He was afraid he might say something he shouldn't at the wrong moment.

It was getting darker fast, and Nam-sik, who was right in front of him, looked a little like a black rock. He spoke in a low voice.

"From now on, we watch the lights carefully. When the guards are changing, the flashlight beams will start waving around. We stay still and wait until the new guards take over and go off on patrol. Whatever happens, don't hurry."

Nam-sik's voice had a sense of authority that made him sound like a bureaucrat from the Workers' Party. With his fists clenched tightly, Yeong-dae licked his lips once and swallowed hard. The palms of his hands started to sweat right away.

Flashlight beams came on around the guard post. There were two of them. The beams gradually moved closer to the next hidden sentry station. The lights waved around wildly and then a moment later, they vanished. They seemed to have gone back inside the guard post. After that, no sound could be heard for some time. The guards seemed to be handing things over to the guards who were there to relieve them. The lights were back. It was the flashlights of the guards who were off duty and heading back to their barracks.

"In a little while, the guards on duty will go on patrol. We have to be careful until they finish their rounds," Nam-sik whispered.

"I got it."

Time passed very slowly. At last, a light came on in the guard post. The guards on duty were going on patrol. For some time, the beams of light wandered here and there, dancing on the surface of the frozen river. The two beams flickered back and forth like fireflies on a sweltering summer night. They stretched long and then shrunk, traced arcs and then angles, came closer and then slinked further away. Yeong-dae's eyes were locked on the lights, and every muscle in his body was tense. The beams peaked from behind the trunks of trees like they were playing hide-and-seek. The moment the lights disappeared into the guard post would be the fateful moment. No matter what, they had to make it. They had to slip like ghosts through a gap between the hidden sentry posts. Yeong-dae wondered why people didn't have wings. He wished he could muffle the sound of his footsteps like a cat. It would be even better if they were invisible. If only they were already in China!

At last, the lights vanished.

"All right, count to ten and off we go. One!" Nam-sik whispered.

Yeong-dae counted to ten with him. *Two . . . three . . . four . . . five . . . six . . . seven . . . eight.* His whole body was trembling. *Nine . . . ten*!

"Okay, that's it. Let's move!" Yeong-dae said as soon as they finished counting.

He took the first step. All they had to do was descend a steep slope and they would be at the river. Afraid he might slip and roll down to the bottom, he moved carefully, one step at a time, testing the ground with his toes. Finally, he was standing right next to the dark surface of the river. The moment he stepped on the river—which looked so black because it was frozen all the way through—he would have to run with all his might. Yeong-dae took a deep breath.

"Now we make a dash for it, OK?" Nam-sik said.

Yeong-dae was about to answer when they heard it.

"Fwee! Fweeeee!"

It was the sound of a whistle blowing. In a flash, Nam-sik was crouched on the ground.

"Get down!" he told Yeong-dae in a whisper.

Yeong-dae dropped down and flattened himself on the ground. He felt like he'd be hit by a bullet if he lifted his head. The shriek of the whistle was getting louder. He raised his head slightly and looked in the direction of the whistle. The sound was coming from below the guard post. Several beams of light pointed across the surface of the lake in several directions.

"Today's not going to work," Nam-sik said. "There are guards crawling all over. Looks like they found some people trying to sneak across at the hidden sentry station downstream from here."

Yeong-dae climbed back up the steep slope. They wouldn't be safe until they reached the place they had hidden during the day. While they were upstream from the guard post, they couldn't relax because of all the hidden sentry stations. If they didn't hurry and hide in the woods, they could be nabbed in an instant if the guards showed up.

Yeong-dae was making his way up the hill when he heard gunshots and fell to the ground. For a moment, all thoughts vanished and a strange whiteness filled his head.

"Yeong-dae! What happened?"

Filled with terror, Nam-sik shook his friend until Yeong-dae slowly returned to his senses and got back to his feet. He was all right. He had been so startled by the gunfire further down the river that he had collapsed. Yeong-dae crawled to the top of the hill. He couldn't tell where anything was in the darkness. He was so nervous that he could barely breathe. No more gunshots could be heard. Downstream by the guard post, the flashlight beams were still waving around wildly.

Yeong-dae caught his breath and sat on the ground. When he took off his backpack, he found that his body was drenched in sweat.

"If we'd tried crossing the river, we would've gotten caught," Nam-sik said after catching his breath. "Where did all of those guards come from? There were so many of them!"

"No kidding! There could be even more guards out tomorrow night. What do we do?"

"Tomorrow night, we have got to cross, and that's final. That means we've got to stay put and wait one more day."

"Nam-sik, where's our hiding spot?"

"We'll know when the day comes. For now, let's rest here."

As the sweat on his body cooled, Yeong-dae began to shiver

violently. Despite the cold, the two boys could not light a fire. The only way they could keep warm was by rubbing their bodies energetically. They took more clothing out of their backpacks and put it on over what they were already wearing.

A little later, the day slowly began to dawn. It was only then that they could vaguely see their surroundings.

The spot where they had hidden for the past three days was right next to them. Frost had dusted the dead leaves with a layer of white. Yeong-dae cleared away the ice-covered leaves. Fortunately, a boulder was there to shelter them from the wind. Yeong-dae pulled some cornmeal out of his backpack.

"Nam-sik, let's have a bite to eat first," Yeong-dae said. He put some of the dried corn kernels in his mouth and started chewing.

Yeong-dae and Nam-sik collected more dried leaves and stacked them higher in the hiding spot. But though they were sitting on a pile of leaves, they kept shivering. They battled the cold by carefully moving to stay in the sunshine. They had to stay where they were and wait until it became night again.

To forget the cold for a while, Yeong-dae thought back on everything that had happened to him. He had no idea how he had managed to survive to the age of twelve. He relived those awful days when his family members had left his side, one by one.

How wonderful it would be if he could go back to when he had been with his mother, father, and his sisters Yeong-ran and Yeong-ok. If the rations had not been cut off—and if he hadn't fallen behind on his kids' work—Yeong-dae would probably have been attending senior middle school[1].

---

1. "Senior middle school" is the North Korean term for secondary school.

Kids' Work

Yeong-dae had been in the third grade. Every day, he had to wander through the fields and hills until the sun sank below the horizon because of what they called "kids' work." Like all students, Yeongdae had a quota of old, worn-out items he was supposed to hand in at school. But no matter how hard he looked, he couldn't find any scraps of metal, pieces of old rubber, or even a single strip of torn paper. As he trudged along, dragging the empty sack behind him, sand would get into the holes of his shoes and chafe his toes.

This time, he had to do whatever it took to get textbooks for his main classes. He had only one option: stealing. He knew it was wrong, but how was he supposed to study without books?

In the beginning of second grade, Yeong-dae had been given just two textbooks. One was for art class, and the other for physical education. He couldn't let that happen again. He was seriously behind on his kids' work, but if he could turn in even half of it, he thought he might be given at least one textbook for one of the really important classes like arithmetic or science.

As soon as Yeong-dae got home, he begged his younger sister Yeong-ok to help him. The rest of the family had gone to the market and hadn't come back yet. That was a bit of luck.

"It's just this once. It's not like I'm trying to buy some ice cream, bread, or cookies," Yeong-dae told her. "If I'm going to study, I've got to have some books. We're just going to do it this one time, and then never again."

Yeong-dae had his sister make a solemn promise that she would never steal again either, and then the two of them waited for it to get dark.

They headed to the factory where the machines had stopped running because there wasn't enough fuel. In front of the factory was a beat-up truck whose doors had fallen off. The truck leaned crazily to one side where the air had gone out of the tires. The moonlight shining on the truck made the scene look even drearier.

"You hide here and watch carefully. If you see or hear anyone, you just hoot like an owl. Got it?"

"OK," Yeong-ok answered in the darkness. "Yeong-dae, don't forget to get my kids' work, too!"

Yeong-dae knelt down and nimbly slid into a small hole in the wall beside the factory gate. The hole was much bigger than his body. He realized that having a little body could come in handy sometimes.

Every time his mother saw him, she would cluck her tongue and mutter about him being just skin and bones. He was a growing boy, she said, but didn't have enough to eat. But Yeong-dae wasn't the only one like that. Both his little sister Yeong-ok and his classmates at school were shorter and skinnier than was normal for people their age.

Children and adults alike would go around all day long looking for junk to pick up, but more often than not they would come home empty-handed. The teachers at school were well aware of this, but even so, they would harass students on a daily basis, telling them to hurry up and hand in their kids' work.

Back when Yeong-dae's big sister Yeong-ran was in

elementary school, the government handed out free textbooks to all students. North Koreans were proud that school supplies and books were provided for them. But a few years ago, students were at a loss when schools stopped giving them new textbooks, never mind pencils and notebooks.

The pencil lead snapped off before you could write a single word, and there were far too few notebooks to go around. Notebooks were made of corn husks or rice chaff, and the writing surface was uneven and ripped all the time. But even notebooks like that were so hard to come by that children nearly always practiced their handwriting in sandboxes. They made the sandboxes by arranging logs into a square shape and filling the middle with sand. Thanks to the sandboxes, the children didn't even need an eraser. They could write something in the sand with their fingers, scratch it out, and then write again.

Since the government was no longer providing many textbooks, people sold used textbooks at the market for high prices. But Yeongdae could do no more than daydream about buying those textbooks.

From first to third grade, Yeong-dae had never once been given proper textbooks. The old books distributed at school had missing pages or were so tattered that you could hardly use them. Students were lucky just to get a full set of these low-quality textbooks.

Yeong-dae crawled into the dark factory and fumbled around like a blind man. The huge machines that came within reach of his fingers didn't budge. He would have been happy just to find a tool made of iron, but couldn't feel anything.

Yeong-dae ran his hands along the floor until they ran into a bulky mass of iron. He cautiously picked it up, but it was too heavy and he dropped it with a clang. He held his breath for some time, afraid that someone might have heard the sound of the iron banging against the floor. He tried pulling the iron forward. It didn't move.

Yeong-dae groped along the floor again. His fingers brushed against some steel wire. When he tried tugging on it gently, he found it was easy to pull toward him. With great care, he coiled the wire up. Just when he was about to go outside, he heard the hoot of an owl.

"Whoo!"

Startled by the sound, Yeong-dae froze in his tracks.

"Whoo! Whoooo!"

Clearly, it was Yeong-ok making the sound.

Yeong-dae spun to face the little hole beside the factory entrance. There was a black shadow moving near the hole. He quickly moved backward and pressed himself flat against the factory entrance, not making a sound. A boy could be heard speaking in a low voice in the darkness.

"Hush! Take anything you can. Nam-sik stole something here and turned it in for his kids' work, too."

"I got it. Just make sure you keep a good lookout."

Yeong-dae's ears were tingling. Nam-sik was an older boy in the neighborhood whom Yeong-dae knew well. Obviously, the boys who had come to the factory to steal something were Nam-sik's friends. After some time, Yeong-dae heard a grunting sound from somewhere inside the factory. Then someone called out.

"Hey! Hurry over here. This is too heavy for me to lift by myself."

The boy who was watching at the little hole came running over to the other boy. The two of them picked something up and then vanished outside the hole.

It was only then that Yeong-dae stealthily carried the coiled steel wire through the hole. Yeong-ok was nowhere in sight. Perhaps she had gone home. Yeong-dae rushed home himself with the wire in his hands. Standing at the door was Yeong-ok.

"Yeong-dae, did you only bring one thing? What about my kids' work?" she asked as soon as she saw him.

"I'm just lucky not to have been caught. All of the iron scraps from the factory had already been stolen. This is all there was, I swear!"

"That's not fair! I got in big trouble with my class captain again yesterday for not turning in my kids' work. Yeong-dae, if you don't give me that coil of wire, I'm going to tell on you for stealing it."

Yeong-ok stuck out her bottom lip in a pout.

At that moment, the other family members came back from selling wood at the market.

"Shh! You hush now. Just try to tattle, and I'll get you back!" Yeong-dae said.

Yeong-dae had not always meant to steal. There was a quota for how much scrap metal, paper, and rubber had to be turned in for kids' work. If that quota wasn't met, not only the students but also the teachers were held responsible. Children stayed in the same classes from the time they started school until they graduated, and those who got behind on their kids' work found that it piled up higher and higher each school year.

In the end, these students had to deal with their kids' work by handing in junk they bought at the market, food such as beans or corn, or even cash. This was impossible for those who had a hard time just finding their next meal; in the end, these children had to drop out of school.

In North Korea, there was a shortage of every kind of material, so hardly anything was thrown away. Cracked pots were soldered up and reused, and torn rubber shoes were patched just like old clothing was and worn again.

The teachers made sure the class captain and the subcommittee head got on the case of children who failed to turn in their kids' work. In other words, kids who failed to meet the quota got picked on by their classmates. For Yeong-dae, getting on the bad side of the class captain or the subcommittee head was worse than a scolding from his teacher.

Yeong-dae couldn't fall asleep as he thought about how far behind he was on his kids' work. His older sister Yeong-ran must have noticed something was up.

"Is something the matter, Yeong-dae? Why do you keep tossing and turning?" she asked quietly.

Yeong-dae kept secrets from his father and mother, but never from Yeong-ran. She was on his side, and she was always ready to listen to what he had to say. In a whisper, Yeong-dae told Yeong-ran about stealing the metal wire. He wasn't about to tell anyone else, though.

"Yeong-dae, I'm sorry I wasn't able to buy you a notebook," Yeong-ran said in his ear, gripping his hand in hers. "If you don't get an arithmetic or science book this time, I'll get you one. Don't steal again. Okay?"

Yeong-dae felt sorry for pestering his sister to buy a notebook for him. She had dropped out of senior middle school and now spent her time at the market. Even so, part of him wanted to be naughty and make a fuss.

"Yeah, how am I supposed to believe that? You already said you'd buy me a notebook, but I'm still waiting. Since you haven't bought me one, I don't even want to practice handwriting in the sandbox."

"Yeong-dae, I'm sorry," Yeong-ran said, looking into Yeong-dae's eyes. "I don't have much money to work with, so a lot of times, I go to the market and can't make anything. Sometime soon, I'm really going to buy you a good notebook. Just hang in there a little longer. No matter how hard things get, you shouldn't steal."

Yeong-dae's eyes spoke for him. *Okay, Yeong-ran. That was the last time. I won't do it again.*

The next day, Yeong-dae went to school early in the morning. He was on pins and needles, afraid that someone would find out that he had stolen the steel wire. When he went to class, he hurriedly turned in the coil of wire. Neither the subcommittee head nor the class captain asked where he had gotten it. If the students didn't reach their kids' work quota, the teachers wouldn't let them go home until long after the sun went down.

At last, it was time to hand out the textbooks. The class captain and the subcommittee head returned from the teacher's room without a single new book in their hands. Yeong-dae was only given a music book and an art book, and he walked home sadly. Once he got there, Yeong-ok hobbled over to him and spoke sulkily.

"I can't go pick the grass for the rabbit. You have to pick my share, too."

"Why should I? How did you hurt your leg?"

Yeong-dae was already annoyed about not getting textbooks for his major classes despite turning in the wire he had stolen, and he felt even angrier when Yeong-ok started whining.

"The subcommittee head told me to dust off the portrait of

the Great Leader because I hadn't turned in my kids' work. It wasn't even my turn to do it," Yeong-ok said, wiping tears from her eyes. "I fell down while I was dusting the portrait, and almost broke my leg. Yeong-dae, do you think the Dear Leader[2] knows that we're having such a hard time?"

Yeong-dae hesitated momentarily and then answered.

"He probably knows. I'm sure he knows."

Even if it wasn't true, Yeong-dae wanted Yeong-ok to feel better.

When Yeong-dae was in first grade, he often had to dust the painting hanging above the chalkboard in the morning. Each time, he was terribly afraid he would fall off the chair.

Picking grass for the rabbit wasn't easy, either. Each year, every student at school had to hand in fur from five rabbits. Since students also had to go around collecting junk for their kids' work, there was never enough time to find grass. The government needed rabbit fur to make uniforms for soldiers. Now that Yeong-ok was in school, Yeong-dae's family had to hand in fur from ten rabbits instead of five.

Yeong-dae left the house with the sack for holding the grass

---

2. The Great Leader refers to Kim Il-sung, founder of North Korea. The Dear Leader is his son and successor, Kim Jong-il.

slung over his shoulder. On the embankments between the vegetable fields, the grass had been pulled up by the roots as soon as it sprouted, and there was nothing left but the dirt and the dust his feet kicked up. The grass was all gone because people in his village used the roots when they cooked porridge.

Yeong-dae was yanking on a dry kudzu vine when a frog hopped out of the mud. He threw down the net and ran after the frog. Each time he thought he had it, the frog kept leaping out of his grasp. He could almost see those tender frog legs, broiled until golden brown, and he started salivating. Just when he had the frog in his hands, it peed and slipped away, leaping down to the field below the embankment. Trying to chase the frog, Yeong-dae tripped and tumbled into the field. His clothes got covered with mud during his fall, the seat of his pants ripped, and he even skinned his knee. He had no idea where the frog had hopped off to. His chest heaving with anger, Yeong-dae pulled up some dried kudzu vine and stuffed it in his sack. When was the last time he had tasted meat? He was terribly upset that he had let the frog get away.

As Yeong-dae neared his house, he saw his older sister and mother coming home from the market. He thought it was strange that they were coming back earlier than normal, when the sun was still far from setting. There was also something strange about the way his mother and Yeong-ran were walking. Yeong-dae's heart sank. What could have happened at the market? Yeong-dae ran toward the house, carrying the sack of dry kudzu vine.

Big Sister

Yeong-ran's face was as dark as a thundercloud. Yeong-dae kept an eye on his mother and older sister as he hurried to stuff the dry kudzu vine into the rabbit cage. Mrs. Lee was giving a lecture to Yeong-ran.

"Families are supposed to stick together through thick and thin!" she said. "You're a young woman now, and before long, you'll be old enough to get married. You can't really mean that you're leaving the house. Please give this some more thought."

Yeong-dae wanted to know where his sister was hoping to go.

"I've been thinking about this for a while, Mom," Yeong-ran said. "Yeong-dae has to keep going to school, and now Yeong-ok's legs have gotten crooked because she isn't getting enough nutrients in her food. I'm still way too young to get married, and I'm not planning on getting married anyway. Didn't you hear the woman? She said I can earn some money and also have as much rice as I want."

"My word, Yeong-ran, how do you know you can trust her about all that? The whole country is starving to death. Why would it be any different somewhere else? I'm definitely not letting you leave, and neither will your father."

Mrs. Lee undid the handkerchief wrapped around her head, dabbed at her tears, and blew her nose with a honk before disappearing into the kitchen.

"Yeong-ran, where do you want to go?" Yeong-dae asked, hoping to hear more about his sister's plans.

Yeong-ran patted Yeong-dae on the head but didn't answer him. When her hand touched his head, Yeong-dae's eyes started tearing up. What would he do if Yeong-ran left? For Yeong-dae, the house felt even drearier when his sister was gone than when his mother was. She was seven years older than him, and she had always been kind to him.

Yeong-ok's eyes had lit up when she heard the word "rice."

"Yeong-ran, you're not going to feast on rice all by yourself, are you? Can't I go with you?"

Yeong-dae felt the urge to smack his silly younger sister on the head, but Yeong-ran wrapped the little girl up in her arms.

"I'm going very far away, Yeong-ok. I'm going to make a lot of money and treat you to as much rice and meat soup as you want. But why are you limping like that? Did you hurt yourself?"

"I fell down while I was dusting the portraits of the Great Leader and the Dear Leader," Yeong-ok said, her face puffy and red from crying. "The subcommittee head made me do it because I haven't been turning in my kids' work. It wasn't even my turn!"

"That's terrible! You really have to be careful. But since you fell and hurt yourself while dusting the portraits of the Great Leader and the Dear Leader, I just know that they'll make you feel better soon. Yeong-ok, the grass porridge may not taste very good, but you have to eat a lot of it, okay?"

As she gave Yeong-ok a pat on the back, Yeong-ran's eyes grew a little misty, too.

Mrs. Lee came out of the kitchen and started trying to reason with Yeong-ran.

"If you bring this up with your father, he's just going to yell at you. Things are so bad here in our country. Don't you think it'll be even worse in another country? If the Dear Leader can't bring us out of poverty, who can? That woman was lying through her teeth when she told you she'd feed you rice at every meal. I'm telling you, there's not a country in this world that has it better than we do!"

Yeong-dae was barely listening to what his mother was saying. He had always been taught that the Great Leader and the Dear Leader were the sun for the people of North Korea. He didn't think this was actually true, though. They told him that the Great Leader and the Dear Leader shone down on the nation with a light brighter than the sun, bringing happiness to all of the people. But somehow more North Koreans were sighing and moaning with hunger each day.

Every day, Yeong-dae's father went to the food distribution center. He wasn't the only one, though. Their next-door neighbors and those down the street had pinned their last hopes on the center. Every day, they waited hopefully for rations, though they didn't know when distribution would start up again. They were told that rations weren't being given out for now, but that it wouldn't be like this forever.

When the workers were told to show up at their factory despite having nothing to do, his father would mutter to himself about how much he hated going. He grumbled about how they were forced to sit there all day long without even getting paid, and how they had to sit through monotonous lectures about the Juche philosophy[3].

"I mean, what's the point of going to the factory when it's not even running?" he would complain. "And no matter how hard you work, what's the point? Since they give us the same rations anyway, why would anyone want to try harder? It'd be better just to go to the market and carry around people's goods for them."

But with the entire country brought to its knees by the lack of raw materials, there was little chance of getting their rations no matter how long they waited. Even so, Mr. Lee waited for the rations, and then waited some more. At the depressing factory, the cold wind moaned in the halls while dust settled on the rusty machines.

In the early winter, when they ran out of corn and roots could no longer be dug out of the frozen ground, Mrs. Lee and Yeong-ran started going to the market. Most of the people there were women. Along with many other women, they put

---

3. Juche is the official ideology of the North Korean regime. Developed by Kim Il-sung, Juche teaches that a country should be politically, economically, and militarily self-sufficient.

all of their household possessions worth any money up for sale. Mrs. Lee brought all of her family's furniture, sparing only the clothes and eating utensils that were necessary for daily survival, and traded them for corn flour. Now that they had run out of items to sell at the market, the house looked strangely empty.

Yeong-dae couldn't remember how long it had been since he'd had rice to eat, even for his birthday or on a holiday. He couldn't even remember the last time he had corn mixed with rice. The very word "rice" had grown unfamiliar to him. He was lucky just to get his fill of porridge—corn porridge, grass porridge, or root porridge.

It was after the sun had sunk in the west that Mr. Lee came back from the food distribution center and tiredly entered the house. Yeong-ran must have been waiting for him, because she started talking as soon as he arrived.

"Father, I've made up my mind to leave home and get a job."

Mr. Lee's eyes nearly popped out of his head when he heard that.

"What? Not *that* again! Didn't I tell you no last time, too?"

"They say a lot of people have already crossed the river, Father. If I go to China, they told me I can eat as much rice as

I want and get a job where I can make a lot of money, too! I promised that I'd go with them."

"You promised? Just who did you make that promise to? Oh, never mind." Mr. Lee turned to his wife. "Honey, what's Yeong-ran going on about?"

"Well, I told her that she couldn't go last time, too, but she doesn't listen to me," Mrs. Lee said timidly, lowering her head. "Since Yeong-ran talked to a woman she met at the market, she's been stubbornly insisting that she's going to leave right away. What am I supposed to do?"

Yeong-dae's father let out a long sigh.

"Yeong-ran, get these silly thoughts out of your head. We have to be patient a little while longer until the Republic can get back on its feet again."

Mrs. Lee nodded in support of what her husband was saying.

"We all have to accept the will of the Dear Leader and wait until the Republic becomes strong and prosperous. We just have to endure some difficulties for a short time along the way. Yeong-ran, the Dear Leader is here with us. What do we need to worry about? Just keep quiet and listen to your father," she said.

Mr. Lee started reasoning with Yeong-ran as well.

"Yeong-ran, don't you know that the harder things get, the more a family has to stick together? Set aside those foolish thoughts and stay here at home. Don't fall for their honeyed words. Do you understand?"

Yeong-ran lowered her eyes and didn't answer.

"Why aren't you saying anything? Don't you hear me?" Yeong-dae's father said. "I'm telling you not to fall for the tricks of those con artists."

But Yeong-ran didn't say a word. Her heart breaking, Mrs. Lee pressed her to answer.

"Yeong-ran, hurry and promise you won't leave!"

With even her mother against her, Yeong-ran burst into tears and ran into her room. Father cleared his throat loudly and left the house.

Yeong-dae had always been taught that no country on earth had people who led better lives than North Korea. Yeong-ran had always told Yeong-dae the same. But what was she thinking now? He wondered what the woman at the market could have said to make Yeong-ran stand up to their father.

As soon as Yeong-ok fell asleep that night, Yeong-ran took Yeong-dae's hand in hers and spoke to him softly.

"This is for you, Yeong-dae. It's a very expensive notebook, just like you always wanted."

Yeong-dae was shocked when he saw the notebook that she was holding out to him. It had a glossy cover, and the pages shone. It looked like it would be perfect for writing on.

"Wow, Yeong-ran! This notebook is great."

"Isn't it, though? Yeong-dae, you told me that you couldn't practice your handwriting because you didn't have a notebook, didn't you? After you've done a lot of practice in the sandbox, try writing neatly in this notebook. When I come back after earning some money, you'll have to show me just how neat your handwriting is."

Yeong-dae's jaw hung open with excitement. He had never dreamed of having a notebook as nice as this. He remembered whining to Yeong-ran every time he practiced his handwriting in the sandbox. His complaint was that he couldn't practice without a good notebook.

"Yeong-ran, where did you get a notebook this good?"

"When I told the woman who's setting me up with a job that I had to buy my little brother a notebook, she got this for me. She said it's really expensive. Listen carefully, Yeong-dae. Even if I'm not here, you have to work hard on practicing your handwriting in the sandbox and then write neatly in the notebook, OK?"

Yeong-dae's chest was pounding with happiness.

"I was planning to get you a math book and science book, too," Yeong-ran said. "I'm sorry I wasn't able to before I go."

"Yeong-ran, are you really going to leave? Didn't Father say you can't go?"

"Hush! Be quiet. I need to leave until the Republic becomes strong again. That way, there'll be one less mouth to feed. I'll be sure to send all the money I make. You have to take good care of Yeong-ok. I'll be thinking of you as I work hard to make money."

Yeong-ran held her brother's hand tightly and didn't let go for a long time. Just then, they heard Father coming back in from outside.

"Pretend you didn't hear any of this," Yeong-ran said. "Hurry and go to sleep. It's late."

"Yeong-ran, what am I going to do if you leave? I don't even have any school books. Who's going to help me with my homework?"

"You have to do it on your own now. You have to work hard even when I'm gone. Studying is important, but right now, what's even more important is not starving and just staying alive. Go to sleep!"

Yeong-ran quickly turned the light off and lay down. Yeong-dae wanted to ask her when she was leaving, but couldn't. He was afraid she might tell him she was going right away.

Yeong-ran called his name once more.

"Yeong-dae, are you asleep?

"No, not yet. What is it, Yeong-ran?"

"Well, if Chang-u happens to come looking for me, ask him to wait for me. Got it?"

Yeong-dae told her he would and closed his eyes again, hugging the notebook his sister had given him. But sleep was a long time coming.

The next day, Yeong-dae's eyes popped open when he heard his mother's voice coming from outside.

"It's Yeong-ran, dear. I don't see her!"

"What did you say? What about Yeong-ran?" His father sounded startled, too.

"When I got up, she was gone. What are we going to do?"

Yeong-dae jumped out of bed and ran outside. His mother was pacing back and forth anxiously.

"Her clothes are gone. Her purse is gone. All of Yeong-ran's things are gone. She must have run away. Goodness gracious, when could she have left?"

"Mother, is Yeong-ran really gone?"

"Yes, she must've slipped out when we were all asleep. Hurry up and find her, dear!"

Mr. Lee hurried to the main road. Yeong-ran had sneaked out of the house while the family was all asleep. Yeong-dae had a vacant stare on his face, and the thought of going to school was far from his mind. Last night, his sister had been trying to say good-bye. He was sorry that he had been too absorbed in the notebook to notice.

Mrs. Lee poured the grass porridge into the bowl and urged Yeong-dae to eat it.

"You're going to be late for school. Hurry and drink this down and then grab Yeong-ok and run on to school. Father will find your sister and bring her back."

Yeong-dae stuffed the notebook his sister had given him deep into his backpack and went to school. But even at school, he couldn't think of anything but Yeong-ran. Was she really going somewhere where she could eat rice and make money, too?

From the time Yeong-dae was a little boy, his sister had stood in for his mother when she went to the farm and had done everything for him. She had been a playmate during playtime, a teacher for his studies, and a mother when it was time to fix a meal. Even when Yeong-ran dropped out of school and started going to the market with his mother, Yeong-dae felt like something was missing. But now she was going to cross the river into China! Just the idea of it made him feel like there was a hole in his heart. Would his sister really make money so that the family could have their fill of rice? At the rate things were going, they wouldn't be able to eat corn, let alone rice, and they might even die of hunger. Some people in their village had already starved to death.

As soon as school was over, Yeong-dae rushed home. His father was standing dumbly in the yard, and his mother was wiping away tears with her handkerchief. It was clear they hadn't found his older sister.

All of a sudden, Mr. Lee stormed into the house. Yeong-dae and his mother followed him inside, where they saw him emerging from his room holding a big bundle of paper and striding purposefully into the kitchen. There was the sternness of a soldier in the way he walked. Mrs. Lee watched her husband, looking dazed.

"It's high time I burned these blasted ration vouchers. Dammit! How many years of my life have I let myself be fooled by them?"

Yeong-dae's father threw the stack of vouchers he had so carefully saved into the fireplace and lit them with a match. A moment later, bright red flames started licking the paper.

Mrs. Lee was taken by surprise.

"For heaven's sake, what are you burning those for? What are we going to do if they start handing out rations again?"

She stuck the poker into the fireplace and started fishing out the burning vouchers. Mr. Lee snatched the poker out of his wife's hand.

"Drop it! What's the point? These damn vouchers will shrivel the flesh right off our bones. We've been counting on empty promises that nobody's going to keep. It would be better to die than to go on living like this. The Great Leader, the Dear Leader, they're all useless. We might starve to death like the others someday. I guess I should start going around gathering herbs, or even picking up scrap metal. I mean, would Yeong-ran have left the house if things hadn't been this bad? Ah, these stupid vouchers!"

His face flushed, he threw the vouchers that his wife had hurriedly pulled out of the flames back into the fireplace.

"Goodness, dear, someone's going to hear you! Anyway,

what's gotten into you today?" Mrs. Lee said, hurriedly shutting the kitchen door and looking around nervously.

"You really don't know what's the matter with me? Yeong-ran has run away from home. How can you even ask me that?"

Mr. Lee beat his breast with his fists and stared up at the sky.

"If I'd known that she was going to run away at night, I'd have told her not to worry about sending money home. I'd have told her just to make sure she gets enough to eat. You should've done more to stop her. She left without preparing anything. She's going to have all kinds of trouble," he said with a groan.

Mrs. Lee said, "I told her not to go over and over again, but she just had to have her way. What could I have done? I hope nothing happens to her while she's far from home."

"When you go to the market, be sure to track down the woman who Yeong-ran went off with. Find out exactly where she's going, along with whether they're really going to give her a job, and if they do, what kind of work it is."

"Okay, but don't think I'm any less upset about this than you. I did everything I could to stop her. What am I supposed to do about her not listening and running away? Now we just have to hope that she'll be okay, that nothing will happen to her," Mrs.

Lee said worriedly.

Mr. Lee was muttering to himself.

"We shouldn't have let a big girl like her loose in the market like that."

Yeong-dae's parents both took a deep breath and let it out slowly.

Whenever Yeong-ran went to the market, she had met friends without her mother's knowledge. A few of those friends told her that they were going to cross the river into China to get a job and make some money. After that, each time Yeong-ran went to the market, she saw a woman who told her that she could get her work. In the end, it seemed, she had gone off with the woman, who had almost certainly given her Yeong-dae's notebook. But there was no way of knowing whether Yeong-ran had gotten work or not when she crossed the river. Every day, Mr. and Mrs. Lee fretted about their missing daughter.

"Make sure that the kids watch what they say," Mr. Lee reminded his wife. "If the Party finds out that our daughter crossed the river, they'll brand us as traitors. If they'd just keep the people from starving, this kind of thing wouldn't happen. Who knows how long our country is going to barely get by like this."

Every time Yeong-dae thought of his sister, he pulled out the notebook she had bought him. He wanted to write in the new notebook right away, but instead he practiced his handwriting even more diligently in the sandbox. He wanted to fill the notebook with very neat handwriting.

After Yeong-ran ran away, his father often raised his voice at his mother:

"Did you go to the market and find out something about Yeong-ran? Didn't I tell you to find out whether she's working or starving?"

Every time Mr. Lee lost his temper, his wife spoke cautiously, as if treading on thin ice.

"But what can I do to find out? I can't find any signs of the people who Yeong-ran used to see. Maybe it's because they all crossed the river to find work, but they've disappeared without a trace. I'm also scared that the Party will notice if I'm too hasty. If only your rations hadn't been cut off, Yeong-ran would never have thought of leaving . . . "

Hearing the word "rations," Mr. Lee flew into a rage.

"Why am I responsible for the rations being cut off, huh? Factories aren't running across the entire country. I want to know why that's my fault. The world is going to hell!"

Whenever his parents started arguing, Yeong-dae would act like he didn't notice, taking his younger sister Yeong-ok outside to the rabbit cage to look after the rabbits or slipping away to be alone. Each time, he missed his older sister dearly.

Two months passed, then three, and before he knew it, summer vacation was right around the corner. Yet his family heard nothing from Yeong-ran. Yeong-dae was picked on time and time again by the class captain and subcommittee head because he hadn't turned in his kids' work for the whole semester. Every day, he waited desperately for news about his older sister. Had she forgotten about her little brother and sister now that she was no longer at home? Maybe she couldn't be bothered to think about her siblings since she had plenty of rice to eat herself. Yeong-dae even started to resent his older sister.

When they started to run low on corn flour, Yeong-dae's father began worrying about what to do. But since he had only worked at the factory, there really wasn't anything he knew how to do. His mother frequently visited the market by herself, but since even corn flour was hard to come by now, the porridge she cooked became a thin, watery soup—and even that was something they could only eat twice a day. Since there wasn't enough to eat, Yeong-ok had trouble walking properly. In the end, she stopped going to school. She found it hard enough to make it to the outhouse and back.

One day, when Yeong-dae thought about his older sister, he wrote in his new notebook for the first time.

I miss you, Yeong-ran.

The good quality paper made the notebook easy to write on. For a long time, Yeong-dae stared down at the sentence he had written. If only he had more notebooks like this, he thought, he could study better, too. He couldn't wait to show his older sister what he had written.

Wandering around looking for work, Mr. Lee headed into the hills, saying he would chop wood to sell.

Every day, his wife went to the market, while Yeong-ok, who couldn't walk very well, watched the house. On the days that Yeong-dae came home late, she would be outside waiting for him.

"You're having a hard time, aren't you, Yeong-dae? My mom gave me this to eat. You have it," Yeong-ok said, holding out a piece of *kkojangtteok*, a cake made by kneading dough from corn flour and steaming it in a big pot.

"Where did this come from?" Yeong-dae said, looking at the

cake.

"Well, Mom got it somewhere. She said I should eat it all since I can't walk right. I thought of you and saved a little. Go ahead and have it."

Yeong-ok's words made the tip of Yeong-dae's nose tingle. His mother had somehow managed to get the corn cake to give to Yeong-ok because she was malnourished, but Yeong-ok had saved some of it for him.

"I don't need to eat it, Yeong-ok. Look at me. I'm able to walk OK, right? Don't worry about me. Eat everything that Mother gave you and hurry up and get healthy."

Yeong-dae held the cake out to Yeong-ok, but she wouldn't take it.

He broke the cake in half. He put half of it in Yeong-ok's mouth and half in his own and then smiled at his sister.

"Yeong-dae, I laughed so hard today because of the kids down the road," Yeong-ok said through a mouthful of cake.

"What happened?"

"The thing is, they said the Dear Leader is a woman."

"They *what*?"

"So when I told them that he wasn't, they made fun of me. They told me I was stupid."

"Why?"

"They asked how a man could have curly hair. They laughed at me because I didn't even know the Dear Leader was a woman."

"Really?" Listening to Yeong-ok's story, Yeong-dae burst into laughter and then nearly choked on the cake.

"So I taught them that the Dear Leader is the son of the Great Leader," Yeong-ok went on.

She didn't have a lot of energy, but Yeong-dae was happy to see her giggling as she talked.

"Yeong-dae, I told the little kids that they shouldn't talk like that to just anyone or they might get arrested. I did a good job, didn't I?"

"Yeah, Yeong-ok. You did a very good job."

Yeong-dae was relieved to see that Yeong-ok seemed to be regaining her strength after eating the cake. If their mother had been there, she might have scolded them for laughing. She sometimes told them not to laugh because too much laughter can work up an appetite.

Strange *Songgi* Balls

After Mr. Lee came back from cutting wood and selling it at the market, he brought back pine wood and started stripping *songgi* from it. *Songgi* was the thin inner bark of the pine tree that could be found by peeling off the outer bark with a knife or scythe. Though Mr. Lee spent all day stripping *songgi*, it hardly added up to much at all, and what he could get was tough and leathery because it was out of season. When he was done, he handed all the *songgi* to his wife, along with a white lump of something else. At first glance, it looked a little like a chunk of ice.

"*Songgi* is supposed to be eaten in the early spring, dear," Mr. Lee said. "Right now, it's tough, so we have to boil some of this with the *songgi* to make it softer. This stuff isn't good for our bodies, so put in just a little bit."

Her lips pressed tightly together, Mrs. Lee took the *songgi* and the white lump from her husband, put them into the pot, and boiled them together for a long time. *Songgi* could be made tender by boiling it all day long and then taking it out of the pot and beating it with a mallet. Afterward, Mrs. Lee mixed corn flour with the *songgi* and cupped it into round balls. Yeong-dae had never imagined that they would be eating balls made from corn and pine bark.

His mother eyed the *songgi* balls doubtfully.

"Honey, is it really okay to put this stuff in here?" she asked her husband.

"Other people said they ate it like that, so it'll be OK. You just added a tiny bit, right?"

She nodded her head weakly.

Yeong-dae wondered what his mother and father were talking about.

"Mother, what did you put in the *songgi* balls?" he asked.

"Ah . . . nothing. Never mind," she mumbled. She looked flustered.

Mr. Lee continued going into the woods to strip off *songgi*, and Mrs. Lee kept mixing it with corn to make balls, adding a lump of the white stuff when she boiled the *songgi*. Yeong-dae was extremely curious about the white stuff that she put into the balls. She seemed so secretive about it.

The *songgi* balls were so tough that they were hard to swallow. One day, Yeong-dae's little sister ran back from the outhouse in fear, crying as she came.

"Mom, I'm—I'm bleeding!"

"What did you say? Where are you bleeding?"

"My butt hurts. It's bleeding," Yeong-ok said with a sob.

Yeong-dae's heart skipped a beat. It seemed like the strange stuff Mother was putting in the balls was finally causing a problem. Yeong-dae was even more scared because he had also seen blood in his stool before, just like Yeong-ok.

"Mother, I don't want to eat the *songgi* balls," Yeong-dae said. "They don't taste good, and . . ."

Yeong-ok cut in to the conversation and started complaining, too.

"Yeah, Mother, I don't want to eat them either. They taste awful and don't go down because they're so tough. Can you make us some rice?"

Hearing these words, Mrs. Lee's face suddenly grew stern. She picked up a big paddle.

"Yeong-dae, get over here!"

Yeong-dae hesitantly went to stand in front of his mother.

"How can you be so childish in front of your little sister? You think I don't know how good rice tastes? Is there anyone who doesn't know that? You think I'm not fixing it for you because I don't know how good it is? Well? You should be patient, if only for your little sister's sake. What are you trying to do, just shooting off your mouth like that? Huh? How do you not see that I'm doing everything I can to keep you from starving? You've got a lot of growing up to do."

Mrs. Lee paddled Yeong-dae hard on his bottom for some time and then threw the paddle to the side. Yeong-dae felt scared. He had never seen his mother like this before.

"I'm sorry, Mother. I won't do it again. I made a mistake. I'm sorry, Mother!"

Yeong-dae was crying now, which scared Yeong-ok, and she began to wail again. Mrs. Lee put her arms around Yeong-dae and cried for some time. It was the first time Yeong-dae had heard his mother crying so miserably.

After that, Yeong-dae ate the *songgi* balls without saying a thing. When they were tough to swallow, he drank some water and gulped them down. Each time he swallowed a bite, he felt like his eyeballs were going to pop out of his head. Still, he couldn't grumble about it tasting bad or being hard to get down. His father told him that, since all the mugwort and other herbs had been picked as soon as they sprouted, more people were going into the woods to strip *songgi*.

After Yeong-dae's family started eating the *songgi* balls, they all had trouble with their bowel movements. They became severely constipated since the food didn't have any nutrients in it and contained hardly anything but fiber. Yeong-dae's mother and father kept doing their best to cook *songgi* balls and feed them to him and his sister. They said they had to eat something, even *songgi* balls, just to keep their intestines from sticking together.

Yeong-dae's father sometimes brought back tender edible leaves that he found. They boiled the leaves to make porridge. The day after eating the porridge, Yeong-dae and his family had diarrhea that was the same color as the leaves. The day after they ate *songgi* balls, their feces were as hard as rock and as brown as tree bark.

They were skipping meals, but they were not allowed to miss the monthly Party lecture. When people came back from the lecture hall, they resented and hated the United States and South Korea with every fiber of their being. The lecture was always about the same thing.

"We have many mountains, Comrades, but we have few fields for planting rice or growing crops. This is why we have to import rice," the speaker would say. "The Dear Leader imports rice for our people, but our enemies in the United States and South Korea shoot at the ships that carry the rice. That's why we must go through such difficult times. If we can just endure this trial, our Republic is sure to become great and powerful."

On days when there was a lecture, people both young and old would grind their teeth with hatred for the enemies of North Korea. Yeong-dae hated them for making his people go hungry, too.

When Yeong-dae was listening to the lecture, he was reminded of the movie *Chosun*, which he had seen once with his class from school. The movie was about a little girl named Chosun from South Korea who had lost her parents in the Korean War and lived in an orphanage in South Korea. There wasn't much to eat at the orphanage, so all of the orphans were malnourished. On top of that, people looked down on Chosun, and she was lonely. Just when she was about to starve to death, she made it to North Korea. In the North, Chosun was able to experience a mother's love for the first time. As she experienced the warmth and love of her homeland, she put on weight and her face grew prettier. When the children in Yeong-dae's class watched the movie, they felt so bad for children in South Korea that they started bawling, and felt proud to have been born in North Korea. But Yeong-dae thought that if Chosun came to North Korea then, she would starve to death right away.

As soon as Yeong-dae got home, he pulled out the notebook his big sister had bought him and began to write.

Yeong-ran, I heard another lecture today. Every time I hear a lecture, I just hate the enemies of our country so much. If it weren't for our enemies, you wouldn't have left us. Yeong-ran, I miss you so much.

Every time that Yeong-dae wrote in the notebook, it seemed like his sister was right there in front of him. She had said she would send money once she got a job. Why had they still not heard anything from her?

Day by day, Yeong-ok's eyes sank further into her face. Her arms and legs became skinnier, too, until her bones could be seen under the skin.

Looking down at Yeong-ok's jaundiced face, Mrs. Lee spoke

to her husband.

"When I was at the market yesterday, I ran into Mr. Song from Tiger Boulder Valley. He told me he'd found a lot of *seogi* mushrooms. Apparently the Chinese will pay a lot for *seogi* mushrooms since they use them in gourmet cooking. If we could just pick some *seogi* mushrooms and sell them, we could feed Yeong-ok something with more nutrients."

"*Seogi* mushrooms? Where did he say he found them? *Seogi* mushrooms are rare, so they're probably really expensive. Why didn't I think of that before?"

"Are you planning to go gather *seogi* mushrooms? They grow on the sides of cliffs, so it's probably dangerous," Mrs. Lee pointed out.

"Our daughter is about to die. Does this look like a time to worry about what's dangerous?"

"Don't go by yourself, dear. Go with Mr. Song."

Mr. Lee clucked his tongue at his wife's words.

"If I want to make any money, I have to get the mushrooms myself. If I split the mushrooms with someone else, it won't amount to much. It might take me a couple of days, so make sure to fix *songgi* balls so the kids don't starve while I'm gone."

Yeong-dae's father seemed to have made up his mind. His

mother was looking anxiously at Yeong-ok, who was growing weaker each day.

"You know that stuff I put in when I make *songgi* balls," she said. "Are you sure it isn't bad for us?"

"You can't make *songgi* balls if you don't put that in, so what choice do we have?"

"Well, I did rinse it off several times, but for some reason I just keep worrying about it."

The next day, Father left early in the morning to head into the woods. People said there were a lot of *seogi* mushrooms on cliffs deep in the mountains. Mother packed some *songgi* balls for Father to take.

Every once in a while, when Yeong-dae was going around picking up junk, he was lucky enough to catch a frog and grill it for Yeong-ok. He wanted to see his sister jump to her feet after she finished eating the frog legs. But frogs were quite rare, and he hardly ever caught as much as a glimpse of one.

A few days later, an older boy named Chang-u came to Yeong-dae's house.

"Hey, Yeong-dae," Chang-u said. "Where did your older sister go?"

Yeong-dae hesitated. He had to hide the fact that his sister had crossed the river.

"Yeong-dae, how could Yeong-ran go off without telling me? You know that your sister liked me, don't you?"

Yeong-dae nodded silently. Chang-u liked Yeong-ran a lot. At first, Yeong-dae had hated Chang-u for liking his sister. But when he learned that she had feelings for Chang-u, too, he delivered a lot of letters between the two of them. Chang-u was the son of the local Party secretary, and he was two years older than Yeong-ran. Not only was he healthy and handsome, but he also had a sharp mind and was an excellent student.

Yeong-dae didn't have any brothers, and sometimes he wished that Chang-u were his older brother. Remembering what Yeong-ran had asked him to do, Yeong-dae thought quickly and came up with a likely story.

"Yeong-ran went to my grandmother's house. She probably won't be coming back for a long time. Grandmother is very sick. My sister asked you to wait until she can get in touch with you."

"Yeong-dae, your sister and I have a special relationship. We've already made plans to get married in the future. You know, don't you?—how much I like your sister, I mean."

Again, Yeong-dae nodded his head, not saying anything.

Chang-u asked him to let him know if they heard from Yeong-ran and then went on his way.

Yeong-dae spent the rest of the day going around looking for junk, but he couldn't find anything worth picking up. At last, he went to the banks of the stream that ran through the next village. A boy his age from that village was already there, holding a sack. As soon as the boy saw Yeong-dae, he yelled at him, pointing at his empty sack.

"Hey you, this is my village. Who said you could come to someone else's village and take all of their junk?"

Yeong-dae smiled sheepishly and held out his own empty sack.

"Well, I went around my entire village and couldn't find anything. I'm empty-handed, just like you!"

"Oh, I'm really in for it. I'm afraid I'm going to end up like Nam-sik."

Yeong-dae's ears pricked up when he heard Nam-sik's name mentioned.

"What about Nam-sik? What happened?"

"Huh, I guess you haven't heard. Both of Nam-sik's parents got hauled off to a concentration camp, and Nam-sik's a *kkotjebi* now. He has to beg for food."

"*Kkotjebi*" was what North Koreans called young boys and girls who had lost their parents and lived on the streets, staying alive by begging or stealing.

"What happened to his parents?" Yeong-dae asked.

"I heard they were listening to radio broadcasts from South Korea. Both his mom and dad got caught. Nam-sik doesn't have anyone to take care of him, so he has to beg at the market. Seriously, though, are we really much different from *kkotjebi*? We have to go around picking up junk every day. It's only a few days till school starts back up, and I'm way behind on my kids' work. Now I'm really going to get it."

Yeong-dae threw down his empty sack.

"You're right. No matter how much we look for junk, we never find anything," he said. "Why don't we just forget everything and go for a swim?"

At Yeong-dae's suggestion, the other boy dropped his net, slipped out of his clothes, and leaped into the river with a splash. Yeong-dae had a blast playing in the water with the boy. The moment he started kicking up the water with his feet, all of his worries disappeared, as if he had returned to the past. In the water, everything was the same as it used to be, but when he came out of the water, he felt frustrated with the world and could do nothing but sigh. Yeong-dae and his new friend splashed water at each other and tried to see who could hold their breath underwater longer. They didn't leave the water until the sun had started to slowly sink behind the hills in the west. Yeong-dae was so worn out that he could barely stand up straight.

When Yeong-dae got home with the empty sack over his shoulder, his little sister said she was burning up. She had gradually been growing weaker, and she wasn't even able to eat. Mrs. Lee laid a wet rag on Yeong-ok's forehead.

"Hang on for just a few more days," Mrs. Lee implored. "When your father brings back some *seogi* mushrooms, I'm going to cook meat stew with some tasty rice. Oh, my poor baby girl."

When he saw his mother taking care of Yeong-ok, Yeong-dae felt guilty for playing in the water.

"Don't be sick, Yeong-ok. I'll catch another frog and cook it for you," Yeong-dae told his sister.

"Yeong-dae, I'm always feeling cold."

Yeong-ok's face was flushed, and she was shivering. They said it was because she had a high fever. His mom's back was bent, too, like an old woman's. There were many times when she went hungry trying to make sure Yeong-ok had something to eat.

Three days passed, but Yeong-dae's father didn't return. Yeong-dae thought he might have to go looking for him.

"Mom, is the place where you gather the *seogi* mushrooms far away?" Yeong-dae asked.

"*Seogi* mushrooms grow around cliffs deep in the mountains. I'm not sure which mountain he went to, so what are we going to do? What if something happened to him?"

His mother's face was pale, and she was trembling.

The fifth day after he had left to pick *seogi* mushrooms, Yeong-dae's father returned, carried on someone's back. It seemed that as he was gathering the mushrooms on the cliff he had lost his footing and fell. They said that one of his legs had gotten caught in a tree when he fell, breaking it. If he had fallen straight down and hit his head on a rock, he would have died on the spot. With his back injured, Yeong-dae's father couldn't even get up. They said he had held out for four days by just drinking water.

Fortunately, Yeong-dae's father had been found by people who worked at the same factory as him and had gone to the hills to gather herbs. They said that if they had gotten there a day or two later, he would have died where he was. The people from the factory took turns carrying Yeong-dae's father and barely managed to make it back home. By then, his broken leg had swollen. When Yeong-dae's mother saw his father, she let out a groan.

"What did I tell you? You hadn't been there before, so I told you not to go on your own but to follow Mr. Song. What are we going to do now? Even if you go to the doctor, there probably won't be any medicine. What can we do?"

Despite her attentive care, Yeong-dae's father slowly lost more energy. As Yeong-dae watched his father anxiously, he worried that he might pass away.

With his mother busy looking after his father, she couldn't go to the market, and they didn't know where their next meal was going to come from. Chang-u had heard the news that Yeong-dae's father had gotten hurt, and every few days he brought over a hunk of cold rice and some dried kernels of corn. Yeong-dae's mother boiled the cold rice to make porridge for his father, and she cooked corn porridge for Yeong-ok and Yeong-dae. She said she was full and hardly ate anything herself.

Day by day, Yeong-dae's father grew weaker, and several days after he returned home, he couldn't even get up. He had no feeling below the waist. He said he thought the nerves leading to his legs had been paralyzed when he hurt his back. He even had to lie down when relieving himself, with his wife cleaning up after him.

On days when his mother went to the market, Yeong-dae stayed by his father's side to look after him. One day, his father spoke to Yeong-dae worriedly.

"Son, I had really wanted to send you back to school no matter what else happened. I'm sorry. You have to at least finish elementary school . . . Even if you can't go to school, you've got to study as best you can in your spare time to gain recognition from the Party. Do you understand? Later, when the situation in our country gets better, you have to go back to school."

"All right, I will. Hurry and get better, Father," Yeong-dae said.

Yeong-dae's father was talking like someone who was never going to get up again. How he missed the father of his childhood, who built sleds and made tops for him. Even when the snow rose to the eaves of the house and the ground was frozen solid, Yeong-dae and his father went sledding all day long. Would that kind of day ever come again?

He was frightened to see how much his father's face looked like a skull, with all the flesh wasted away. Where could his older sister be? She had no way of knowing their father was in such a dire state. If only she were there with them, he would feel much stronger.

A few days later, his father could no longer urinate, and his whole body began to swell up. He wasn't able to keep the porridge down or drink any water. Finally, two months after being brought back home, he died.

Mother

Yeong-dae couldn't believe that his father was dead. Lying there on the floor, his father looked just as if he were sleeping. It seemed like any minute he would open his eyes, leap to his feet, call Yeong-dae to him, and say how well he had slept. Yeong-dae realized that he would never get to hear his father's voice again. He felt as if he had a big, gaping hole in his chest.

Mrs. Kim, the woman who lived down the road, was the first to arrive. She had heard Yeong-dae's mother weeping. As soon as Mrs. Lee saw her neighbor, her sobbing got even louder.

"It's all my fault that my husband died! When I told him that *seogi* mushrooms sold for a good price, he went off to pick some, and then. . ." Her voice was interrupted by sobs. "How are we supposed to survive now?"

"You have to stay strong for the kids," the neighbor said. "What other choice do you have?"

"Why is life so hard? What am I going to do? I don't even have the money to buy a bottle of wine![4] I feel so bad for this husband of mine."

"How could our country have gotten into this state?" the other woman said, wiping away tears. She clucked her tongue. "Well, it looks like you'll have to boil some lopseed in water and use that instead of wine. You can't hold a funeral with just plain water and no alcohol, can you?"

"You're telling me to use water boiled with lopseed instead of wine?"

"That's right. With everyone on the verge of starvation right now, where are you going to get wine? Someone starved to death in the next village a few days ago, and I heard they used water boiled with lopseed for the funeral. I'll go pick some lopseed right now, so get ready to boil some water."

In the past, the government would send bereaved families ten

---

4. Alcohol plays an important part in Korean funerals.

won[5] and one *mal*[6] of rice to hold a funeral, but this practice had stopped recently. A little while later, the neighbor lady brought some lopseed she had picked. Yeong-dae's mother washed off the lopseed and quickly set it in the pot to boil. Putting lopseed in water and boiling it produces a mildly sweet liquid. The two women filled the glasses with this liquid instead of wine and held the funeral.

They didn't even have a coffin, so men in the neighborhood rolled up the body in a straw mat, lifted it onto a *jige*[7], and moved it to the public cemetery. There was no shroud to wrap the body in, so they left Yeong-dae's father in the clothes he was wearing when he died. When his body was put in the ground, Yeong-dae and his mother wept. Yeong-dae couldn't believe that he'd never see his father again. His mother was so overwhelmed and crying so much that they were barely able to finish the funeral.

"How am I supposed to go on? Yeong-ran isn't even here, so how can I keep the kids from starving? Someone tell me that!"

---

5. The North Korean currency is known as the *won*. The same name is used for the South Korean currency.

6. *Mal* is a unit of volume. One *mal* is about 18 liters, or 4.8 gallons.

7. A *jige* is an A-frame strapped on a person's back for carrying heavy or bulky objects.

Mrs. Lee said.

The other woman helped Yeong-dae's mother get to her feet and tried to reason with her.

"Mrs. Lee, you've got to think about the kids and stay strong. You have to keep going one way or the other."

Supported by her neighbor, Yeong-dae's mother barely managed to return to her house. When Yeong-ok saw her mother, she burst into tears. Yeong-dae tried to comfort his little sister.

"Yeong-ok, stop crying," he said. "Soon enough, I'll grow up and smash our enemies into pieces for you."

While Yeong-dae put on a brave act when he was with Yeong-ok, he was scared at night, too. There wasn't much electricity in the country, so they couldn't keep the lights on for long. After dark, visions of his father—shriveled up like a mummy—kept flashing before his eyes. Some days, when he went into his room, he seemed to see his father lying down, staring back at him with huge eyes.

Every time this happened, Yeong-dae pulled out the notebook that his sister had bought him.

Dad died, Yeong-ran. Mom's sick, too. How are we supposed to keep going now? Where are you? I'm so scared. I'm scared about everything, about Dad not being here, and about how we're supposed to survive in the future. Have you forgotten about me? When are you going to come back? I can't wait to see you, Yeong-ran.

After he finished writing the letter to his sister, Yeong-dae felt a little calmer. When would North Korea become a "strong and powerful country"? What was the Dear Leader doing? How long would the Great Leader—the people's everlasting sun—just watch his people starve?

Yeong-dae and his mother made a long trip to the forest to chop wood to sell at the market. His mother's body was weak, and she said her back hurt from carrying around bundles of firewood. She had suffered from back problems a long time ago, and now that she didn't have enough to eat and was doing hard work, her old illness flared up again. Before long, she could hardly walk. Yeong-dae had no choice but to go to the market by himself and find something—anything—to eat.

"Mom, this just isn't going to work. You need to lie down and get some rest. I'm going to go to the market and beg if I have to," he said.

Yeong-dae no longer had anyone to rely on. He was terrified at the thought that his mother might weaken, collapse, and never get back up again, just the way his father had.

The boy decided to strap on a *jige* and work as a porter carrying things at the market. Most of the people who hired porters were Joseonjok[8] merchants. Since there weren't very many of them, there were no positions open for Yeong-dae. The merchants tended to prefer older, stronger porters; Yeong-dae was young and looked frail.

Yeong-dae couldn't bear to go home empty-handed. His mother and Yeong-ok would be lying down, waiting to see what he was bringing back for them. He wasn't sure what he should do. Finally, he mustered up his courage and walked toward the bakery. As he gazed at the loaves of bread, his mouth began to water. Left without any other options, Yeong-dae made up his mind to beg for food from the woman who ran the store. But it wasn't easy to get the words out. After hesitating for a long time, he finally managed to open his mouth.

"Excuse me, can you please help me?"

He said it so quietly that the words didn't even make it past his lips. He coughed loudly and spoke again. This time, his

---

8. Joseonjok is a term used for Chinese citizens who are ethnically Korean. They are the descendants of Koreans who immigrated to China generations ago.

voice was still low but at least it could be heard.

"Excuse me. Can you help me out, please? My mother and little sister are dying. Please?"

The woman at the bakery clucked her tongue and handed him a piece of bread and bread crumbs. Yeong-dae fought back the urge to eat them all then and there. Instead, he took the bread back to his house. After breaking the bread into two pieces, Yeong-dae gave one to his mother and stuck the other into Yeong-ok's mouth. His mother refused to accept it and told Yeong-dae to eat it.

"Mom, I ate at the market. I'm telling you, I'm full."

But his mother didn't believe him.

"Mom, why don't you believe me? I really did eat at the market."

With tears running down her face, Mrs. Lee split the piece of bread in two and put half of it into Yeong-dae's mouth.

"Yeong-dae, why don't you have my piece, too," Yeong-ok said as she watched. "I'm just going to eat half as well."

"Yeong-ok, go ahead and eat it," Yeong-dae said somewhat sharply. "I won't be able to rest easy until you eat a lot and become healthier. Stop thinking about things like that and just eat the bread. OK?"

Yeong-ok nodded her head wearily.

When Party leaders learned that many North Koreans were going hungry, they announced the beginning of the People's Food Saving Campaign. Yeong-dae thought that the Dear Leader was finally paying attention to his people. He thought that the Party was trying to save food and ration it out to the starving.

Party officials also threatened severe punishment for anyone caught during the campaign stealing from storehouses where produce from the collective farms was kept. They seemed to be making the threat out of fear that thieves might break into the storehouses.

Quite a few people stole food from the storehouses since the food had been produced through the collective effort of the people. These people didn't consider it stealing when they secretly went off with some food from the storehouses. Since the food was all produce that the people had grown on their farms, they didn't think of it as belonging to someone else. They simply thought that they were taking back food that they had grown.

The Party said it could do nothing about ordinary people starving to death, but that soldiers must be fed. They called this the military-first policy. Even when Yeong-dae was so hungry that he was afraid he might faint, he believed he had to endure even this so that the fatherland could be reunited.

Chang-u would sometimes come by with a hunk of cold rice and ask about news from Yeong-ran. Each time, Yeong-dae lied to him that she couldn't come back because his grandmother had been bedridden for some time.

On one visit, Chang-u noticed that Yeong-dae's mother was too sick to do any physically demanding work, and he took pity on her. A few days later, he found a job for her at a food storehouse. He said he had barely managed to get her the job after begging and pleading with his father, the local Party secretary.

Yeong-dae felt an incredible sense of gratitude to Chang-u. He even thought that it would be nice if Yeong-ran came back quickly so that she could marry him.

After Yeong-dae's mother started working at the storehouse, she brought back a handful of corn kernels each day. It was barely enough to make porridge for a single meal, and Yeong-ok wasn't able to digest the kernels very well. Yeong-dae kept going to the market, and when he was lucky, he would carry goods for someone and get to eat a bowl of soup.

One day, about two weeks after his mother started working at the storehouse, Yeong-dae got home from the market later than usual. When he entered the house, corn porridge was simmering in the kitchen and a little sack full of corn flour was sitting in the corner.

"Mom, did they give you this at the food storehouse, too?" he asked.

Caught by surprise, Yeong-dae's mother dropped the spoon she had been stirring the porridge with.

"No, Yeong-ran sent it to us," she said.

Yeong-dae was thrilled to hear his older sister's name.

"Yeong-ran? Did you hear from Yeong-ran, Mom? Where is she?"

His mother didn't say anything in response. As she stirred the corn porridge, her facial expression was as hard as a lump of lead. Yeong-dae's nostrils were twitching with the savory smell of the corn porridge. He thought that even Yeong-ok would be able to digest it. That evening, Yeong-dae slurped down so much delicious corn porridge that he thought the spoon might wear out.

But for some reason, his mother's face was still troubled. Yeong-dae wrote another letter to Yeong-ran that evening.

Thanks, Yeong-ran! Mom made some tasty porridge with the corn flour that you sent. I haven't had porridge like that in a long time. I'd much rather you be here with us, even if that means we can't eat rice and only get corn porridge. Yeong-ran, when is the Republic going to become a strong and powerful country? These days, more and more people are starving to death in our village. I believe that the Great Leader and Dear Leader aren't going to abandon us, but I'm getting a little scared. How are things where you are? If things are this bad here, I bet they're even worse where you are. Yeong-ran, please pray with me that our country will become strong as soon as possible. Take care of yourself, Yeong-ran.

After Yeong-ok ate the corn porridge, her health improved noticeably. Yeong-dae asked his mother about Yeong-ran.

"Mom, why didn't we hear anything from Yeong-ran until now? If she had sent us some corn porridge earlier, Father wouldn't have had to die. Didn't she say anything about when she's coming back?"

"Yeong-dae, you better not say a word about your sister outside of this house," she said.

"Mom, Yeong-ran said she was going to buy me a math book and a science book. Wouldn't it be OK to ask Yeong-ran to help me pay for my kids' work just this once? If she sends us the money, I could go to school again. . ."

All of a sudden, his mother got mad at him.

"Yeong-dae, I'm telling you not to talk about your sister anymore! Do you understand?"

Yeong-dae thought that his mother was angry because she felt guilty about Yeong-ran for some reason. He wondered why his older sister had sent corn flour but not a single letter.

Shortly before the end of summer vacation, Yeong-dae hung around school, wishing he could take classes again. But he got discouraged when he thought about all of the kids' work he still had to do, and school felt very far away. Yeong-dae went around diligently, looking for scrap metal and old paper.

"Not even a *mal* of rice would be enough to pay for all the kids' work you owe," his mother told him. "I want to send you to school, too, but we don't have a choice. I'm sorry, Yeong-dae."

When she saw his pouting face, she kept speaking.

"The teachers at school are busy working at the market. Do you think they'd be able to do a decent job teaching? If things keep going like this, it's only a matter of time before the whole school shuts down. You can't count on school. Study by yourself when you have some spare time."

Yeong-dae decided to plead with his mother one last time.

"Mom, I really want to go to school. Even Father said I have to finish elementary school at least. Can't you ask Yeong-ran to send some money so we can pay for the kids' work that I owe? Looking at the corn flour she sent, it seems like she's earned a lot of money . . ."

Yeong-dae's words trailed off when he saw his mother's face. She blew up at him again.

"I already told you to stop wasting your breath talking about things like this. Do you think I feel any better about this than you do? I want to send you to school, too. You don't know anything about how it feels for a mother not to be able to send her son to school!"

Yeong-dae was upset with his mother. He packed his backpack and put all of his pencil stubs in the pencil case. As he stared silently at his bag, he started to cry. That night, he heard his mother sighing again and again.

The next day, his mother went to work at the food storehouse as usual. Yeong-dae waited until late in the evening, but she still hadn't come back. Yeong-dae started to feel nervous. After putting his little sister to sleep, he hurried to the storehouse to find his mother. Just when Yeong-dae reached the front of the storehouse, he heard a man's voice coming from inside the collective farm's storehouse—even though the lights were off. Yeong-dae crouched beside the wall of the storehouse and stayed still. The man's voice was deep, and he seemed to be in a hurry. Yeong-dae held his breath.

"Shh! I think someone's coming. We've got to make this fast!"

Next, Yeong-dae heard his mother's voice.

"Tonight is the last time. Hurry and give me the money like you promised."

"Okay," the man answered. "This is the last time for us, too. We have to keep this a secret until our dying day."

"All right," Yeong-dae's mother replied. Her voice was shaky.

Two black shadows came into sight. They were carrying something and moving quickly. Whatever they were carrying looked rather heavy, and they were grunting as they moved. After waiting for the two figures to disappear into the distance, Yeong-dae cautiously approached the storehouse. His heart leaped into his throat. His mother, who was about to shut the storehouse door, jumped in surprise when she saw her son.

"Hey, what are you doing here?"

"Well, it was late at night, and you weren't home . . ."

Yeong-dae's mother shut the door quickly, as if someone were after her.

"Let's get going," she said. "And don't ever show up here again."

Something seemed odd to Yeong-dae about how much of a rush his mother was in.

"Mom, who were those people back there?"

His mother was so surprised that she stopped in her tracks.

"Hush! You don't need to know. Come on, let's go."

Yeong-dae still felt that something was wrong.

"Mom, is everything really OK?"

His mother lost her temper and snapped at him.

"Why do you keep sticking your head into grown-ups' business? This isn't something you need to worry about."

Yeong-dae was unable to ask any more questions. His mother didn't say a single word for the rest of the walk home. After taking Yeong-dae into the house and locking the door firmly behind them, she pulled out some paper money from her pocket.

"Yeong-dae, this money is for paying for the kids' work you're behind on."

The money that she was holding out to him would have been enough to buy more than half a *mal* of rice. Yeong-dae was so shocked that his mouth hung open.

"Mom, so a little while ago, those . . ."

"Yeong-dae, put those foolish thoughts out of your mind. We got this money from your sister. You're going back to school tomorrow, all right?"

"Mom, when did you see Yeong-ran? Are you sure that she really gave you the money?"

"What's the matter with you? Don't ask me anything else. Is that understood?"

His mother's face was so frightening that Yeong-dae couldn't ask anything else. He wanted to believe what his mother had said, but he just couldn't. He hurried back to his room and pulled out his notebook.

Yeong-ran, I'm so nervous that it's killing me. There's just something weird about Mom. Why in the world have we not heard from you? My handwriting is neat now even without practicing on the sandbox. I can't wait to show it to you. Yeong-ran, please get in touch with us.

Yeong-dae had put his notebook in his backpack and was about to fall asleep when his mother came into his room. She ruffled his hair.

"Yeong-dae, I'm sorry," she said, and started to sob.

It was obvious that she had lied to him.

Yeong-dae tossed and turned all night and didn't wake up until his mother came into the room.

"Yeong-dae, you have to hurry and go to school. Get up now. Come on!"

He got ready for school quickly, with his mother pushing him.

"As soon as you get there, give the teacher the money, OK?" she said as he left the house.

Yeong-dae nodded and made his way to school. Now, he had no choice but to do as his mother said. As soon as he got to school, he handed the money to his teacher.

"Sir, my mother said she will pay the rest a little at a time. Please let me attend school again."

The teacher's face suddenly hardened, and he fixed Yeong-dae with his gaze.

"Yeong-dae Lee, where did you get this much money? I heard that your father passed away."

Yeong-dae hesitated, unsure of how he should respond.

"Fine," the teacher said at last, not asking any more questions.

"Tell your mother to pay the rest as quickly as she can."

Yeong-dae was lucky. He had always felt like a debtor when he came to school, but now he could hold his head high.

The teacher told the students that starting that semester, he would only be teaching the morning classes. He said he had to sell noodles at the market in the afternoon. After class, Yeong-dae was about to head home when the teacher called him over.

"Yeong-dae, it seems that things are looking up for your family. You're going to have to help me out a little," the teacher said. "Tell your mother that I need her to buy a stove to use in the classroom this semester. Our old stove wore out, so we sent it to the scrapyard. It's going to get cold soon, and we're in trouble. We need a stove, and a fire in it, to keep you children warm as you study."

Just as the teacher said, no stove could be seen in the classroom. Every time they had added wood to the old stove, sparks had flown out from the bottom where the iron had rusted through. It looked like the old stove had finally been taken to the scrapyard. Yeong-dae hadn't even paid for all of the kids' work he owed, and now he was supposed to buy a stove! Yeong-dae was outraged. There was no way he could tell his mother about this.

Yeong-dae quickly made his way home. If he hung around school any longer, he didn't know what else they might ask of him.

A few days later, he was once again coming home from school when he saw a car parked outside his house. Standing by the car were strangers wearing the uniforms of the secret police. Yeong-dae felt a hollow feeling in his stomach, and he began walking faster. He kept tripping over his own feet.

When he was nearly at the house, he heard the sound of Yeong-ok screaming from inside. He could also hear his mother wailing. Yeong-dae ran frantically into the house. His mother was on her knees in front of a uniformed police officer. Yeong-ok was on the floor next to her, crying. The officer kicked his mother with his boot, and she rolled around on the floor in pain. Yeong-dae's hair stood on end.

"Mom! What's going on?" he said.

When Yeong-dae's mother saw him from where she lay sprawled on the floor, her face contorted.

"Yeong-dae . . ." she said, sobbing.

"Mom! What is it? What on earth is going on?"

When Yeong-dae remembered what he'd seen a few nights ago, his throat seemed to tighten.

"Mom! Mom!"

No other words would come out of his mouth. The officer screamed at Yeong-dae and threatened to knock him down.

"She's capitalist scum, stealing the country's food. You're a little capitalist, too. Get out of my way!"

Yeong-dae felt as if something had given way inside, as if his heart had dropped with a thud into the pit of his stomach. It was clear to him that the money that Yeong-dae had given to his teacher at school had come from stealing from the food storehouse. He remembered the sack that the men had hauled off, groaning under its weight. The sack had been full of food from the storehouse that his mother had secretly sold. Yeong-dae hated himself. This had all happened because he had foolishly begged his mother to send him to school.

The police officers handcuffed his mother and took her outside, with Yeong-dae following behind. They put her in the waiting car. Two men whom Yeong-dae hadn't seen before were in the car, and their hands were cuffed as well. Yeong-dae cried and called for his mother. She was begging the police officer standing outside the car for something. After a moment's hesitation, the officer responded, both to her and to the other two men.

"All right, everyone, let's get something straight. People who lay their hands on food in the storehouse during the enforcement period for the Food Saving Campaign will be punished severely. You're going to be held accountable for the crimes of everyone who's been stealing from the food storehouse, do you see? You're going to be made an example of."

As soon as the police officer finished speaking, Yeong-dae's mother called to him. Yeong-dae ran to her side of the car. His mother stretched her arms out through the open car door to hug Yeong-dae, but she was in handcuffs.

"I'm sorry, Yeong-dae. Take Yeong-ok and go to your grandmother's house. Do you understand, Yeong-dae?"

She was crying so much that she could barely get the words out.

"Mom! Mom, this can't be happening."

"Yeong-dae, I'm sorry. I'm so sorry, Yeong-dae!"

"All right, that's enough!" the officers shouted as they dragged Yeong-dae away from his crying mother and slammed the door shut.

"Get out of the way," one of the officers said. "Hey, I said move it!" They pushed Yeong-dae away from the car. His mother was banging on the window with her handcuffed hands. He could see her calling his name through the glass. The engine rumbled to life, and he watched helplessly as the car drove away. As Yeong-dae numbly walked back into the house, he hated himself so much for having nagged his mom about sending him to school.

"Yeong-dae, where's Mom going? Why are they taking her away?" Yeong-ok asked with bewilderment.

As Yeong-dae looked at his little sister, the future seemed bleak.

"Yeong-ok, Mom wanted to send us to school, so she went to the food storehouse and . . ." He couldn't finish what he was saying.

What would happen to his mother now? He couldn't imagine life without her. He could live without going to school, but how could he live without her? Had she stolen from the food storehouse knowing that she'd be arrested? Yeong-dae sobbed as he looked at the portraits of the Dear Leader and the Great Leader hanging on the wall.

"Great Leader, Dear Leader! Please forgive my mother. The only reason she did it was because the government stopped giving us rations. That's why my father died, too. Dear Leader, why do you pretend not to see all of your people who are starving to death? Great Leader, Dear Leader! You've gone too far. Please give me back my mother. Please!"

After bawling in front of the portraits for some time, Yeong-dae finally collapsed to the floor in exhaustion.

Grandmother's House

Yeong-ok kept crying and asking Yeong-dae to take her to her mother.

"Yeong-dae, what are we going to do now? When is Mom coming back?"

"Yeong-ok, Mom will be back soon. Stop crying and let's wait for her."

"No! I want to see Mom now! Take me to her!"

Yeong-ok fell to the ground and flailed her legs as she cried. On the inside, Yeong-dae was scared and nervous, too, but he couldn't cry in front of his little sister. He picked her up and set her back on her feet.

"Please, don't cry, Yeong-ok," he said.

Why did the Great Leader leave his people on their own? If he just looked after the lives of his people, this kind of thing wouldn't happen. To Yeong-dae, the days when he went to school singing "We Have Nothing to Envy in the World" felt so very far away.

The sky is blue, and my heart is glad. Let the accordion play!

I have unending love for my homeland, where people live together in harmony.

Our father is the Great Leader Kim Il-sung; our home is in the arms of the Party.

We are all true brothers and sisters. We have nothing to envy in the world.

The lyrics of the song that came to his mind seemed indistinct, like a dream.

It wasn't until late that night that Mrs. Kim, the woman who lived in the house down the road, cautiously came to see them.

"I can't believe something like this has happened! Your mother is in big trouble since she got caught during the enforcement period. But anyway, Yeong-dae, how are you going to get by now? How can little children survive in this harsh world?"

"Mom did it because of me. She did it because I kept

pestering her to send me to school," he told the woman through his tears.

She clucked her tongue.

"Yeong-dae, your mother was having a hard time since she started making *songgi* balls to keep you fed," his neighbor said. "She cried and cried when she put lye in with the *songgi* and boiled it. But what else was there to do? If you didn't even have that to eat, you would all have starved. There she was complaining to me about how there was no point living like this, and now she can't even watch her children starve to death. I thought there was something strange about that corn porridge . . ." She clucked her tongue again.

Yeong-dae protested when he heard this.

"No, that's not true," he said. "Mom told me that my older sister sent the corn flour."

"I thought so, too. If only it were true! Your mother must have been taking some food from the storehouse out of fear that the two of you would starve to death, but she just couldn't bring herself to tell you that she had stolen it. At any rate, you really don't know where Yeong-ran went?"

Yeong-dae shook his head weakly. To think that the white lump that his mother had used each time she made the *songgi* balls was lye! He felt goose bumps rising on his skin. If he had known it was lye, he wouldn't have eaten it.

The other people in the village were nowhere to be seen. Maybe they were afraid they might suffer the same fate if they got too close to Yeong-dae's house. Even Mrs. Kim only stopped by at night, when no one could see her, before hurrying off again. The people in the village were gradually starting to act strangely, too. Once, they had shared everything with others, but after people started starving to death, the old ways gradually disappeared. Yeong-dae was scared of crossing paths with the villagers.

Chang-u stopped by a few times and said his father was in an awkward situation because of Yeong-dae's mother. That made sense, actually. Chang-u's father had felt sorry for her and given her a job at the food storehouse, only for her to steal corn flour just when the authorities were cracking down on theft. Time and time again, Chang-u said he needed to see Yeong-dae's older sister Yeong-ran and asked Yeong-dae if she was really at his grandmother's house. Yeong-dae said she was. Chang-u pointed out that there were just two children left at the house and demanded to know whether their grandmother was more important than their house. Before he left, he asked Yeong-dae to come find him when his sister came back, whenever that might be. Yeong-dae really wanted to ask Chang-u to find out what had happened to his sister, but he couldn't tell anybody that she had crossed the river.

Now that he thought about it, it was after his mother had brought home the corn flour that she had started to get angry at him for no good reason. She had always taught him to live honestly even if he was poor. How could she have decided to steal from the food storehouse? But if it hadn't been for the corn flour that his mother brought home after his father passed away, Yeong-ok might have starved to death. Both Yeong-ok and Yeong-dae had recovered their strength when they started eating corn porridge.

Could his mother have decided that she would rather become a criminal than watch her children starve to death? Trying to pull himself together, Yeong-dae got out his notebook.

Yeong-ran, they took Mom away. Dad is dead and Mom is gone, too. Where are you? Yeong-ran, are you still alive? I want to see you, even if it's just in my dreams.

Yeong-dae thought that the first thing that he'd ask his sister when he saw her was why she hadn't contacted them all that time. Every day, Yeong-ok kept crying about how much she missed her mother.

Yeong-dae wished that the things that had happened over the past few days were just a dream. He didn't even feel like getting up. It seemed like all of the beliefs he had held on to for so long were dropping away, one by one. Neither the Great Leader nor the Dear Leader listened to what he had to say. It seemed like such a long time since he had looked up at the sky and really believed that the Great Leader, the sun of the people, was watching over them. He didn't even have the energy to comfort Yeong-ok, who just kept crying.

What had made North Korea, a worker's paradise, change like this? Did the Great Leader and the Dear Leader know of the pain of the people or not? Even after Yeong-dae had quit going to school, he had sworn allegiance to the Great Leader and Dear Leader in front of their portraits in his house every day without fail. But since his mother was taken away, he felt no desire whatsoever to bow to them in the morning.

The third day after Yeong-dae's mother was taken away, Mrs. Kim came by the house again.

"There are families that are going hungry all over. I wish that the people in the village could pitch in to help you out, but the more time goes by, the worse things get. In addition to that, people are saying bad things about your family. They are calling you a bunch of capitalist traitors. Even people who want to help out aren't able to step forward. What are we going to do with you?"

"But why do they call us capitalists?" Yeong-dae said. "My mother isn't a capitalist!"

The woman patted Yeong-dae on the back.

"Yeong-dae, why don't you go stay with some relatives? Don't you have any relatives living around here?"

It was only then that Yeong-dae remembered that his mother had told him to go find his grandmother. Glancing down at Yeong-ok, who looked like she was about to faint, he returned to his senses. His mother had been arrested for stealing food so that he could go back to school. He couldn't just sit here and cry like this.

"I think I should go to my grandmother's house," he said.

"That's right," the woman said with sadness in her voice. "Much longer like this and both you and your sister will starve. Go on to your grandmother's house."

Yeong-dae remembered his older sister, and his throat went dry.

"There's a favor I'd like to ask," he said. "If my sister Yeong-ran comes back, please don't forget to tell her that we went to see my grandmother."

"All right, I'll do that," she said. Looking at Yeong-dae's sister, the woman added, "You're really in trouble. Yeong-ok is so weak!"

Yeong-dae and Yeong-ok set off for their grandmother's house right away. Their maternal grandmother lived in a seaside village on the Eorang River. Once when Yeong-dae was younger, he had gotten a travel pass with his family and boarded the train bound for the village where his mother's family lived. This was his second trip there.

A lot of children were begging at the train station. They looked like they hadn't washed their faces for several days, and their filthy hair clumped together. The children held out their hands to passersby and asked for money. Yeong-dae stared at them. He thought he was lucky. At least he had a grandmother he could go to.

There was hardly any room to move on the train. People fought just to get a spot on the roof. There were even people riding inside the train bathroom. How could there be so many people? Where were they going? All the people on the train looked like refugees. Only later would Yeong-dae learn that they were on their way to visit relatives to get food. Another reason the train was packed with people was the inadequate supply of electricity. This meant that the trains couldn't run very often. When they did run, they were crowded with passengers who had missed earlier trains.

Staying alert to make sure he didn't lose his grip on Yeong-ok's hand, Yeong-dae somehow managed to find a seat next to the bathroom. Normally, the trip from Kilju Station to his grandmother's house at the Eorang River would take six hours, but the train kept stopping.

People said a person could ride the train without a travel pass since the entire country was a mess because of the food shortage. Still, the train attendants sometimes checked for tickets. Three times, Yeong-dae was caught without a ticket. Twice, he barely got permission to stay on the train by begging with tears in his eyes. Some attendants took pity on them when they saw Yeong-ok and looked the other way.

The third time they were caught, the attendant unceremoniously yanked Yeong-dae and Yeong-ok off the train and gave them a lecture. If they got on the train one more time without a travel pass, the attendant said, they would be really in for it. But they sneaked onto the train again anyway.

After three days, the two children reached the neighborhood where Yeong-dae's grandmother lived. Helping his exhausted little sister totter along, he walked slowly toward his grandmother's house.

In the past, the neighborhood where his grandmother lived had seemed beautiful, but there was nothing beautiful about it anymore. Around the Eorang River were stagnant pools of black water, and it was hard to breathe because of the awful smell coming from the factory where they made heat-resistant materials.

The steel mill looked like it had been closed for a long time. In the yard were machines that had rusted over and a beat-up three-wheel truck, crouched down like some kind of monster. Yeong-dae could also see people in rags begging.

It was starting to get dark when they finally got to their grandmother's house. Yeong-dae knocked on the door, thinking how happy she would be to see them.

"Grandma! It's Yeong-dae. Grandma!"

Yeong-dae kept calling, but no one answered for a while. Finally, his aunt—the wife of his mother's brother—cracked open the door and quietly asked who was there.

"Auntie, it's Yeong-dae. Yeong-dae Lee!"

His aunt was surprised to see him.

"Good grief, Yeong-dae, what brings you here? Where's your mother? Why are you two here by yourselves?"

Not sure what he should tell his aunt first, Yeong-dae started crying. Inside the house, he couldn't see his grandmother, his uncle, or his cousins.

"Where's Grandma? Did she go somewhere?" he asked.

Yeong-dae's aunt held Yeong-ok close as her eyes welled up with tears.

"Your grandmother passed away a week ago. She died all of a sudden, and I've been too preoccupied to try to contact you. My husband was arrested, too . . . But anyway, I can see that something happened to your family as well. That's true, isn't it?"

Yeong-dae was shocked to hear that his grandmother had died.

"Grandma died? How?"

Throughout the long journey, he had been looking forward to his grandmother giving him a big hug. All of his strength seemed to be leaking out of his body.

"Yeong-dae, your grandmother starved to death," his aunt said, sighing. "She'd been sick since last year, but we weren't able to feed her properly, let alone get her any medicine. It's been a long time since your uncle was taken away after he got caught ripping off parts from the machines at the steel mill and selling them. We might starve to death someday, too. But never mind that, Yeong-dae. Where's your mother and father? Why did you and your sister come by yourselves?"

Yeong-dae remembered noticing on his way over that the steel mill had been shut down. His uncle had worked there. If the steel mill was closed, it meant that his uncle had stopped getting rations, too.

Yeong-dae told his aunt everything that had happened. As she listened to his story, she kept wiping the tears off her cheeks.

"What are you going to do? If only Yeong-ran would come back. Since you haven't heard from her even once since she left, she might've been sold."

Yeong-dae was startled by what his aunt had just said.

"Huh? What do you mean, 'sold'?"

"I've heard that some young girls in our village were sold, too. As more people cross the river, bad people take young women from our country and sell them to Chinese farmers. If you haven't heard from Yeong-ran even once, that might've happened to her, too."

Yeong-dae shook his head firmly, not wanting to believe this.

"No way! That couldn't have happened to Yeong-ran."

"You said you haven't gotten any news from her, not even once. There hasn't been any money, either. If she'd gotten a job, why wouldn't she have gotten in touch? But anyway, what am I going to do about you two? Yeong-ok looks like she's going to fall over any minute." Yeong-dae's aunt clucked her tongue and continued. "I already have enough trouble of my own, so I can't take care of the two of you as I should. What am I going to do?"

Yeong-dae's aunt held Yeong-ok in her arms and kept clucking her tongue. Yeong-dae decided to stay with his aunt only until his little sister's strength returned.

The next day, Yeong-dae left Yeong-ok at his grandmother's house and walked alongside the Eorang River. On the street, he saw people dressed like beggars lined up in front of the ration distribution center, hoping to get something to eat. Though it was a long time since any rations had been given out, they would stand in line all day, clutching their ration vouchers, until it got dark. Tears stung Yeong-dae's eyes when he remembered how his father had burned his own stack of vouchers in the oven.

Yeong-dae saw children his age scrounging for food at the market. As soon as they found something that looked edible, they would run off with it. They were called *kkotjebi*. He'd never seen any until now. Thinking of his friend Nam-sik, Yeong-dae watched the children for a long time. He was afraid that, before long, his life would be no different from theirs.

Yeong-dae sat down on the bank of the Eorang River and stared absentmindedly at the water flowing past. It wasn't the pure blue that it had been, but it still brought to mind memories from the past.

The summer of the year that Yeong-dae started kindergarten, he and his family had gone to his grandmother's house. He thought of the time he went swimming in the Eorang River with his male cousins. His older sister Yeong-ran sat on the levee next to the river to watch the boys' clothing while Yeong-dae and his cousins fearlessly plunged into the deep water. Waiting by the river, Yeong-ran would get anxious if Yeong-dae was even just a little late coming out of the water. He was full of daring even as a little boy, and he would hold his breath underwater on purpose to give his sister a scare.

His father had been fishing a little further down the river.

His grandmother was gathering *chamoe* melons in the field, while his aunt was steaming *kkojangtteok* cake. When she was finished, she called the children over to eat it. Those happy days seemed like a dream to Yeong-dae. He could almost see his father over there with his fishing pole. He could almost see his grandmother hurrying over, calling him as she came, with a basket on her head full of green melons speckled like a frog.

Yeong-dae sat there staring vacantly until his stomach started growling. Not until the sun was low on the horizon did he come plodding back to his grandmother's house.

His aunt was out somewhere. When she stepped over the threshold carrying some rusted metal and old paper that she had picked up, she sighed tiredly.

"There are so many people out there picking up scraps. This is all I could find, even though I was out all day," she said. "It isn't enough to make ends meet, I'm running low on corn flour, too. How am I supposed to survive? I have no idea what will become of me."

Yeong-dae realized that he couldn't stay with his aunt much longer. She didn't have any more food than he did.

"Auntie, I'm going to go home now," Yeong-dae told her a few days later.

"Even if you go home, there's no one there," she said. "What are you going to do? But you know, I was thinking of leaving here and going to my parents' house, too. I hadn't been able to make up my mind because of you two. My parents live right by the sea, so I should be able to keep food on the table by selling clams that I find."

Yeong-dae's aunt clucked her tongue and told him she was sorry. He nodded his head tiredly to indicate he understood. Now he had to take Yeong-ok back home. If they went home now, how would they survive? They had already sold all of their home's furnishings. What could he do to make ends meet? Things were looking desperate. Seeing his facial expression, his aunt muttered to herself.

"Kids can survive by begging in the market. They say that Sunam Market in Chongjin is so big that there are lots of *kkotjebi* there. If you don't want to starve to death, you have to put your nose to the grindstone. The Republic had better become that strong and powerful country they're always talking about soon."

To Yeong-dae, it seemed that his aunt was telling him to become a *kkotjebi* if that was what it took to stay alive. He couldn't impose on his aunt's good nature any longer. He had to go home right away.

"I understand, Auntie. I'm going to leave tomorrow," he said.

Yeong-dae felt that leaving quickly was the right thing to do for his aunt.

The next day, his aunt hugged Yeong-ok and stroked her back for some time, fretting over her health.

"At home, at least you'll be able to sleep comfortably. I've packed you some dry corn kernels and corn flour," she said. "If I had more to spare, I'd give you a lot, but I wasn't able to pack more than a tiny bit. I feel so bad about it. Grit your teeth and make the best of it, all right?"

Yeong-dae's aunt accompanied the two children as far as the train station, where they said their good-byes. Around the station, many people were lying on the ground. They appeared to be too weak with hunger to even get up. Roving bands of *kkotjebi* also went around in bands, sniffing the air like hungry hounds. Only their eyes glittered in their dirt-covered faces.

The train journey to the village where Yeong-dae's grandmother had lived had taken three days. But on the way back, the train halted on the tracks for three nights and only moved in fits and starts. It took Yeong-dae and his sister five days to reach Kilju Station.

Since Yeong-ok hadn't eaten much else, she had trouble digesting the kernels of corn. They gave her a bad stomachache, and she barely managed to make it to the village with Yeong-dae's help. Yeong-dae kept imagining that his mother would come bustling out of the house to meet them when they got home. He pictured her asking if they had had a good trip, and whether their grandmother was doing well. Or maybe his older sister Yeong-ran had finally come home and would run out as soon as she saw them.

When he first caught a glimpse of his house in the distance, Yeong-dae couldn't believe his own eyes. Only the shell of the house remained. It was obviously the house that he had grown up in, but nothing was left but the frame of the structure. Yeong-dae was so shocked that he plopped down on the ground right where he was. There was no strength in his legs, and he couldn't stand up. Yeong-ok sobbed as she looked at the strange house.

"Yeong-dae, why is our house like that?"

Yeong-dae was in such a daze that he couldn't even cry. He somehow made it to the house, though he could hardly remember getting there. From up close, the house looked just like a skeleton stripped of all its flesh. The door had been ripped from its hinges, and the posts on either side were standing forlornly. Even on the roof, just the big beams were left. All of the smaller pieces had been torn off. Only the walls and floor remained intact. Clearly, everything had been taken away for firewood. The kitchen was even more of a mess. Broken furniture was strewn across the floor, and not a single plate was in one piece.

How could this have happened? There was hardly anything left of the old house where Yeong-dae and his family had lived together. In the kitchen, Yeong-ok called for her mother and cried.

The chill autumn wind swept through the empty house. Yeong-dae and his sister went into the bedroom when it got dark, but the stars in the sky could be seen through the gaps in the roof. Even the bedding, which was lying scattered around, was largely ruined. Yeong-dae spread tattered clothing on the floor and had Yeong-ok lie down. He had no idea what he ought to do, or how to go about doing it. It was hard enough for him to try to calm Yeong-ok when she cried. When the night grew late, his neighbor Mrs. Kim came to see them.

"Yeong-dae! Yeong-dae, are you there? Yeong-dae!"

The moment Yeong-dae heard the woman's voice, he started

crying.

"Mrs. Kim, how did my house get like this? Who did this to it?"

"Don't get me started!" she said. "People broke into your house and started going off with everything because they said you were capitalists, and I couldn't stop them. I just watched helplessly. I was afraid they'd treat me like a capitalist, too, if I got in their way."

Yeong-dae remembered the police officer kicking his mother right in front of him.

"Yeong-dae, you should've stayed at your grandmother's house," Mrs. Kim said. "What did you come back here for?"

Yeong-dae told her about what his aunt had told him.

"But Yeong-dae, you can't stay here," she said. "People have all become weird. I think it's because they have nothing to eat and are starving. They've lost their minds, trying to get in good with Party officials just to get an extra kernel of corn. It's like they've forgotten how to see and think. When it gets light, leave here and go somewhere else, anywhere else. For goodness sake, the world has become a scary place, and who knows what will become of it. I'm sorry, but I must be out of my mind if I'm telling you children things like this."

Before the sun came up, Mrs. Kim hurriedly made her way back to her own house, as if someone was on her trail.

Yeong-dae didn't know where his mother had been taken, but he wanted to go there. He didn't even have to see his mother. He felt that he would be able to do something if he could just get close to the internment camp where she was being held.

The next morning, after telling Yeong-ok to stay put and wait at home, Yeong-dae went looking for Chang-u. Chang-u was happy to see Yeong-dae, assuming that he had brought some news about his older sister Yeong-ran. But when Yeong-dae instead asked Chang-u to tell him which internment camp his mother was being held at, Chang-u shook his head.

"Yeong-dae, your mother stole food during the enforcement period for the People's Food Saving Campaign," Chang-u said. "They sent her to the internment camp where they put the worst criminals. It's not the kind of place you want to go. Once you're in, you don't come out."

Yeong-dae was stunned to hear that people were never let out of the internment camp.

"Chang-u, are you saying I can never see my mother again?"

Chang-u nodded his head, his lips in a thin line. The last image of his mother rose before Yeong-dae's eyes. Even when the police officers were driving her away, she'd never stopped calling Yeong-dae's name. In a moment, tears formed in his eyes. Chang-u nudged Yeong-dae toward the door.

"Run on home before my father sees you," he said. "If you hear from Yeong-ran, be sure to have her come find me, OK? Tell her that I'm waiting for her."

Yeong-dae went home. He felt bitter about heaven, the Great Leader, and the Dear Leader.

"Yeong-dae, where did Chang-u say Mom is? We can go see Mom, right?" Yeong-ok asked Yeong-dae, who was full of gloom.

"He said she's somewhere very far away. She's so far away that we can't go see her."

"So we can't see Mom anymore?"

Yeong-dae couldn't tell her the truth. He couldn't tell her that they'd never see their mother again.

"He said she has to stay there for a very long time. We can't go see her right now. Yeong-ok, you can be patient even when you miss Mom, can't you?"

Yeong-dae couldn't meet Yeong-ok's eyes as he asked her this, so instead, he pretended to look at the mountains in the distance. Yeong-ok grabbed Yeong-dae's hand.

"Sure, Yeong-dae. You better not cry when you miss Mom, either!" she said.

Yeong-dae barely held back the tears as he nodded. He felt even worse for Yeong-ok now that she was talking like a grown-up instead of acting like a baby. He rummaged through the house and gathered anything that might be useful. All he could find was a battered pot and clothes that looked more like rags. If they had even a hoe, they could have dug up kudzu roots, but not a single piece of metal was to be seen in the house.

Yeong-dae hurried out of the house with Yeong-ok right behind him. He found himself walking toward the public cemetery where his father was buried. At the cemetery, Yeong-dae bowed before his father's grave and patted down the dirt with his hand.

Father, I heard that Mom will never get out of the internment camp. Now it's just Yeong-ok and me. Where should we go now? You're just lying here . . . I'm so scared. Yeong-ok is sick every day, and we have nothing to eat. Father, what am I supposed to do all by myself with you just lying here like this?

Yeong-dae spoke in a low voice, afraid that Yeong-ok might hear him. His little sister unwound the scarf from her neck and laid it on their father's grave.

"Yeong-dae, I'm worried Father will get really cold. I want to cover him up with this."

Yeong-dae wanted to tell her not to, but the words didn't come out. He sat by the grave silently until the sun began to shine brightly the next morning. Yeong-ok was trembling, her lips blue. Yeong-dae got up quickly. He picked up the scarf on the grave, wrapped it around Yeong-ok's neck again, and led her out of the cemetery.

Sunam Market

To get from Kilju to Chongjin, Yeong-dae and his sister had to pass by their grandmother's village and continue traveling north for quite a ways. His aunt had said that Chongjin was a pretty big city and that there was plenty to eat at the market. As autumn advanced, he was starting to worry that it would get colder as they went further north. When the train passed the station near the Eorang River, Yeong-dae kept finding himself gazing out the window. He wanted to feel his grandmother's warmth one last time.

When they got closer to Chongjin, the train was so packed with people that there was no room to move. Like Yeong-dae and Yeong-ok, many people were without a travel pass. Yeong-dae had simply jumped on the train with his sister without any concrete plan.

On the train, they munched on dry kernels of corn for every meal until their teeth, gums, and even chins ached. When they became *kkotjebi* and wandered around the marketplace, would they be able to find food? Would Yeong-ok be able to make it? Yeong-dae's head was so full of worry that he could barely sleep at night.

At last, one week later, they arrived at Chongjin. The square in front of Chongjin Station was overflowing with people. There were people lying on the ground all over, and many others were standing around, waiting for someone.

When a group of *kkotjebi* went by, Yeong-dae stared at them for a long time, lost in thought. From now on, he realized, he would have to live like those children.

Yeong-dae asked a woman with a bundle on her head where Sunam Market was. As it happened, she was heading to the market herself, so he and his sister tagged along after her. Yeong-ok often fell behind, and Yeong-dae was forced to stop and wait for her again and again.

They finally were getting closer to Sunam Market. First, they started to see people who had pitched tents and were selling things. Once they entered the market, they found it bustling with all kinds of merchants who were selling a wide variety of goods: noodles, bread, rice, medicine, fruit, and even seeds.

The market had a little bit of everything. There were even dried toads and snakes, which people considered health foods. Since the beginning of the food shortages, frogs and even grasshoppers had vanished from Yeong-dae's village, and they hadn't seen a single snake. All of the snakes had been caught by hunters since snakes were believed to be a powerful tonic. Yeong-dae guessed that all of those missing animals were gathered together there at Sunam Market.

At the stall of a rice merchant, Yeong-dae saw sacks of rice with strange writing on them. Certain sacks had the words "Republic of Korea"[9] on them, and others were written with letters he couldn't read. He thought it must be English. The place was crowded with so many people coming to shop, people done shopping and leaving the market, and people waiting for somebody that it made Yeong-dae's head spin.

As he gawked at the sights around him and held on to his sister's hand, a group of children rushed past him like a

_____

9. This is the official name of South Korea.

tornado. They were *kkotjebi*.

Like the ones he'd seen before, eyes glinted in unwashed faces. One boy was wearing clothes that were too big for him. Another had covered his body with tattered rags that might have been clothing once. There was even a child wearing a shirt missing one sleeve. There seemed to be four or five boys in the group. The biggest boy ran ahead of the rest and skillfully snatched a bundle that a woman was carrying. He untied the bundle and tossed it back to the boys following him, and the bread in the bundle spilled onto the ground. The other boys got down on all fours and hurriedly picked up the bread, stuffing it into their mouths. The biggest child, who must have gone off somewhere, could no longer be seen. He seemed to be the leader of the group. In a flash, the *kkotjebi* had eaten all of the bread on the ground and ran off in the direction that the big boy had vanished.

Yeong-dae walked quickly after the fleeing children, with Yeong-ok struggling to keep up with him because of her shorter stride. After running for a while, the group of children reached their destination, which was in an out-of-the-way place. The boy who looked like their leader was already there. He was taking something out of a crumpled bag and putting it into his mouth when he saw the two newcomers. His expression turned menacing. A scowl twisted his dirt-covered face, and he stared at the two with a hostile look in his eyes. Frightened by the boy, Yeong-dae and his little sister hurriedly backed away and left the way they had come.

On their way back to the marketplace, Yeong-dae ran into another surprise. He saw someone lying in a dark alley, but the person wasn't moving at all. Next to the prostrate figure was an old woman in rags. She was squatting down, staring with vacant eyes at the people passing by.

Yeong-dae approached the person who was lying down. It was an elderly man. A few strands of his greasy hair lay across his forehead. A fly had landed next to one of his deeply sunken eyes. His hands, covered in dried mud, looked like the floor of a rice paddy that had cracked in a drought. The old woman sitting next to him stretched her hands out to Yeong-dae and muttered something he couldn't understand. Yeong-dae was scared, and he and Yeong-ok left in a hurry.

Were the two people husband and wife? Was the old man already dead? Did this mean that people could starve to death even in a market with an abundance of things to eat? The image of the old man and woman seemed to hover before his eyes.

When Yeong-dae and his sister got closer to the market, they saw more bodies lying on the ground. Children boldly took the shoes and clothing from these bodies and ran off with them. When Yeong-dae saw this, his entire body shook like a leaf. He didn't want to let Yeong-ok see people ripping clothes off the dead. A chill ran down his spine as he turned away. He was afraid that the bodies would rise to their feet and start following him.

Getting deeper into the market, the two began to smell the aroma of fried foods wafting through the air. At once, their mouths began to water. On both sides of the street, hawkers were selling bread sticks, donuts, and other snacks. Yeong-dae played with the money in his pocket, but he passed by without buying anything. Yeong-ok couldn't digest food very well. If he fed her greasy food, he was afraid that her stomach problems would just get worse.

After they'd been walking for some time, several children suddenly came running from behind and shot past them. A female merchant chasing after them and yelling finally came to a halt and cursed at them.

"Damn you, you sneaky little vermin! You think you can steal bread like that? I just can't make any money because of these children."

The boys kept running, with their cheeks stuffed with the stolen bread. Another woman who was selling goods in the next stall over clucked her tongue as she watched the woman coming back after trying to catch the *kkotjebi*.

"You know, it's hard not to feel sorry for the children, too. They're still growing, and they should have someone to love them at their age. Instead, they have to live like beggars without any parents or siblings," she said.

That very night, Yeong-dae knew that he'd have to find where the *kkotjebi* slept and stay with them. He'd heard that the *kkotjebi* found shelter under bridges or in the woods, so he went looking for a bridge. When he found one, there were people already underneath it, sitting in the more comfortable spots. Yeong-dae slowly scanned the area beneath the bridge, looking for some empty room. There was nowhere that he and his sister could squeeze into. He guessed that so many people were there because they'd be protected from the elements.

Yeong-dae went over to a spot where a girl was sitting by herself and glanced around. The strange girl, who looked younger than his sister, was staring at Yeong-dae and Yeong-ok with big eyes, not saying a word. Her face, which was black as soot, looked as if it hadn't been washed in some time. Yeong-dae sat down next to the girl, and Yeong-ok plopped down on the bare ground at once, saying her legs hurt. The girl didn't say anything. After opening up the bundle, Yeong-dae decided that he'd prepare a place for Yeong-ok to sit first and then get some water for boiling corn porridge.

There were heaps of trash and filth on the banks of the stream that emitted a horrible stench. Yeong-dae followed the course of the stream for some time until he found clean water and then filled his battered pot from the stream. The pot, which he'd brought from home, was the only dish that he and his sister had. After returning to their spot by the bridge, Yeong-dae barely managed to get a fire started with trash and sticks that he'd scrounged around for. He stirred the corn flour into the water and started boiling the porridge. It smelled absolutely delicious.

Just then, a group of *kkotjebi* approached Yeong-dae and his sister. Their clothing was so dirty that it smelled bad just to look at it. Nearly all of them were barefoot. One of the boys, who was a little bigger than the rest, came right up to Yeong-dae. The boy was blind in one eye.

"Hey, what do you think you're doing here? We don't have

room for the likes of you."

The boy spoke in a very rough voice. Yeong-ok was frightened, and she scrambled to her feet. Yeong-dae had no choice but to beg for help.

"We just sat down because my little sister's sick. We won't bother you, we promise!"

The one-eyed boy glanced down at the pot briefly and raised an eyebrow.

"You won't get anything for free," he said. "You weren't planning on eating this delicious food by yourself right in front of us, were you? Song-hwa, I'm going to treat you to something tasty."

The girl who'd been sitting by herself was the boy's little sister, Yeong-dae figured. He felt a small sense of relief. He thought that if this boy was capable of taking care of his sister, he might understand that Yeong-dae had to take care of Yeong-ok, too. When the porridge was done cooking, the boy snagged the bowl and shoved Yeong-dae to the side. As quick as that, Yeong-dae toppled over and sprawled on the ground. The one-eyed boy poured some of the porridge into a bowl that his sister pulled out from somewhere. Soon, all of the children in the group were suddenly holding out little bowls that they'd been hiding under their ragged clothing. There were round gourds and dented aluminum pots, and one child was even holding a wooden bowl that had been sliced in half. These, it seemed, were the *kkotjebi*'s food bowls.

It didn't take long for the children to swallow the entire bowl of porridge. Yeong-dae felt anxious. In the blink of an eye, the porridge that he'd cooked for Yeong-ok had vanished down the throats of the wrong people.

"You can't do this! I have to feed my sister Yeong-ok."

Even before Yeong-dae had finished speaking, the other boy flung the empty pot to the ground.

"If you want a spot next to us, hurry and cook some more porridge!" he snapped. "Otherwise, don't ever show your face around here again."

The one-eyed boy was more terrifying than a Party leader. Worried that he might get punched if he tried resisting, Yeong-dae hurriedly bent down to pick up the pot. But a boy who was smaller than Yeong-dae got to the pot first. He wiped the porridge that was stuck to the pot with his finger and put it in his mouth, licking off burnt porridge and the black filth on his finger. At this, the other children standing around came close and licked the rest of the porridge off the pot.

Yeong-dae picked up the empty pot and went to the water's edge. Tears were pouring from his eyes. When he was about to fill the pot with water, he saw his own dirty face reflected in the water. He decided to wash his face first. After quickly washing away his tears, he filled the pot with water and headed back to where Yeong-ok was waiting. When he was nearly there, the one-eyed boy and the other *kkotjebi* were rifling through Yeong-dae's bundle. Yeong-dae dashed over and seized the bundle. When he grabbed it, the little corn flour that was left spilled all over the ground.

"Let go! You can't take this! Please stop!"

Yeong-dae yelled and pleaded at the same time. The one-eyed boy swung his fist at Yeong-dae's cheek, and stars exploded across Yeong-dae's vision. Yeong-dae lost his footing and fell on top of Yeong-ok. Startled, Yeong-ok began to cry. Lying face down, Yeong-dae wrung his hands to beg for mercy.

"Please, don't do this. This is all I have. Please!" Yeong-dae begged, crying.

Just then, another *kkotjebi* slowly walked toward where Yeong-dae was lying on the ground.

"What's all this?" the newcomer shouted.

He spoke in a deep, gruff voice. Yeong-dae dared not raise

his head for fear he'd be beaten again. He heard the deep voice again.

"Give him a break. He's in the same boat as all of us. Don't you feel sorry for him?"

When Yeong-dae lifted his face to wipe away the tears, there was a boy standing in front of him who looked familiar, as if he'd seen him before. Yeong-dae rubbed his eyes and kept staring at the boy. Then it came to him like a flash of lightning: it was his friend Nam-sik. He was saved!

"Nam-sik, that's you, isn't it? Nam-sik?" he said.

The boy with the deep voice looked down at Yeong-dae on the ground. Yeong-dae started crying again.

"Nam-sik, can you help me please? Yeong-ok is really sick."

"Huh? You know this guy?" the one-eyed boy asked.

At last, Nam-sik recognized Yeong-dae, too.

"Yeah, he lived in the village next to mine," he said, and then turned to Yeong-dae. "How did you make it all the way here, eh?"

Yeong-dae felt that everything would be OK now that Nam-sik was here. Nam-sik looked at Yeong-ok and clucked his tongue with concern.

"How's she going to last the winter with a body like that?

Dead or alive, you should've stayed home. What did you come here for? *Kkotjebi* like us aren't even worth calling alive. We're just trash blowing around. Trash, I said."

After Nam-sik showed up, the one-eyed boy and the other *kkotjebi* became better behaved. Perhaps it was because Nam-sik was much taller than the one-eyed boy. Nam-sik seemed to be the leader of the group.

"What's this? You made him give you some corn porridge to let him into the group?" Nam-sik asked the one-eyed boy.

"I hardly had any of it! But right now, he's the richest one of us all," he answered, pointing to Yeong-dae's bag. "Look at this. He's got corn flour and hard corn kernels."

Without saying a word, Yeong-dae stirred more corn flour into the water to make Yeong-ok some porridge. When the porridge was done cooking, he gave a little to Nam-sik and the one-eyed boy before feeding Yeong-ok. The one-eyed boy told him that his real name was Geun-bae. His sister Song-hwa, it turned out, was mute.

Kkotjebi

Nam-sik became a sort of teacher for Yeong-dae, telling him what he had to do to live as a *kkotjebi*.

"Children aren't the only people who live like this. There are also young men who don't have anywhere to go and old people, too. But no matter the age, we all have to beg for our meals. Anyway, if you're going to get by as a beggar, there's an important rule you always have to keep. As soon as you get your hands on some food, you have to stuff it into your mouth, and fast. Food isn't really yours until it's in your belly, you see. If someone snatches some food out of your hand, all the effort you went to is wasted."

Yeong-dae thought of Nam-sik as his teacher. Could they

really survive by eating scraps of food they found on the ground? Yeong-dae was bewildered about everything.

"Yeong-ok's body is too frail for her to steal anything," Nam-sik said, seeming to read Yeong-dae's mind. "Instead, you two should go to restaurants that sell noodles or soup. You can beg for leftover broth that customers don't eat and feed Yeong-ok that."

"You mean there are customers who don't finish their food?"

"Sure! People with money come to the market to buy things, too," Nam-sik said. "Oh, right. Yeong-ok could probably pick up cigarette butts."

Yeong-dae was taken aback by that.

"Cigarette butts? Why would you pick them up? What would you do with them?"

Yeong-dae was amazed by Nam-sik's explanation. There was no cotton in North Korea, so people resorted to removing the filters from the butts and using those instead. Nam-sik said there were even people who just went around looking for cigarette butts. Yeong-dae didn't want to make his sister pick up cigarette butts.

Starting the next day, Yeong-dae took his sister to places that served food. They would wait around in front of a restaurant and keep an eye out for anyone who looked like they had some money. Each time a customer went into the restaurant, Yeong-dae desperately hoped that they'd leave some food, no matter how little it was. But most customers drank every bit of broth from the bowl before they left. For several days, Yeong-dae was only able to beg for a little bit of broth.

But after a few days, he figured out how it worked. Most people with big builds ate all of their food. The people who left food behind were generally women, particularly women who were younger and skinnier. Some women would feel sorry for Yeong-ok when they saw her staring at them as they ate and left some noodles for her. When that happened, Yeong-ok wouldn't eat all of the leftovers but called Yeong-dae over and split them with him.

One day, the two of them were loitering around a shop that sold rice cake. While the shopkeeper was busy helping a customer, a *kkotjebi* grabbed a handful of *chaltteok*[10] cakes and made his getaway. The woman running the shop shouted and came running after him. Yeong-dae could see the boy hurrying to stuff the cakes into his mouth as he ran. But

---

10. *Chaltteok* is a kind of cake made with sticky rice.

after going a few steps further, he began coughing and fell to the ground. Appearing out of nowhere, a group of *kkotjebi* swarmed over the fallen boy, grabbed the cakes from his hand, and ran off. On the ground, the boy was trembling and flailing around. He kept trying to cough something up, and his face had turned a shade of blue. It looked like he was choking. The owner of the shop, who had finally arrived, turned the boy over and pounded him on the back. But the boy kept twisting and turning as if he couldn't breathe. In no time at all, a crowd of people from the market gathered around them. Yeong-dae's body was shaking as if he were that *kkotjebi*. A short while later, the boy stopped moving. Nam-sik, who was standing behind Yeong-dae, started speaking.

"He tried eating the cake too quickly, and it got stuck in his throat. Even so, he must have died happy, since he was eating rice cake. Yeong-dae, you need to be careful, too. Stuff food down your throat, and you could choke and die like that. Well, let's get going. If we keep watching, we'll just feel worse about our own situation. Off we go."

Nam-sik grabbed Yeong-dae by the hand and dragged him off. For several days, Yeong-dae couldn't erase the last sight of the dead boy from his head. Some days, the boy even appeared in his dreams. One time, Yeong-dae woke up in a cold sweat when he gazed down at the face of the fallen boy in his dream and realized that the face was his own.

When the group of children had trouble finding food, they would pick clover and chew on it. Anything that a rabbit could eat, a person could eat, too. Yeong-dae thought of the rabbits that he'd raised. It seemed that his lot in life was even worse than a rabbit's. Each time they saw a kudzu vine, they pulled it up, so the vines didn't have a chance to grow. On days when there was really nothing at all to eat, they would go to the hills on the edge of town and scoop up dirt to eat. At first, Yeong-dae didn't think he could eat dirt, but when he put it in his mouth, he realized that it was better than starving.

Rain meant a slow day at the market. On days like that, the ground was soft, so the group would go around the fields to dig up grass roots. When they happened to find bindweed, the fat roots were as welcome a sight as meat would've been.

The frogs seemed to have vanished. Even in the summer, no one could hear frogs croaking. It was clear that if a single frog started croaking, the *kkotjebi* would descend on it like a swarm of bees. Since the grass was all pulled from the ground before it could grow, there weren't any insects in the fields, either.

Yeong-dae did not understand why Yeong-ok's belly kept swelling even though she wasn't getting enough to eat. Even just running for a short time would leave her short of breath and make her face turn yellow.

After the weather suddenly became colder, there was a noticeable decrease in the number of traders at the market. It gradually became harder to find anything to eat, even at the market.

One day, Nam-sik told the group that he had a good idea.

"You know, even *kkotjebi* can't just pick up and steal food all the time," he said. "A lot of trains go through Chongjin. What we're going to do is steal lignite[11] from the train cars. If we sell lignite, we can buy bread, or even noodles."

The talk of stealing shocked Yeong-dae.

"What do we do if they catch us?" he asked.

"Listen, how much lignite do you think kids like us can steal anyway?" Nam-sik said. "The station attendants are people, too. It's not like they'd kill us even if we did get caught. We just have to be clever enough to steal without getting caught. We'll go on a dark night when they're all sleeping. In the daytime, we

---

11. Lignite, also called brown coal, is the cheapest kind of coal.

can beg from the passengers on the train. There'll probably be people who'll throw us something to eat from the windows."

The train station at Chongjin was a large one that nearly all the trains going northeast or southwest passed through. A lot of trains that carried lignite from the coal mines would stop there, and when there was a power outage, they would stay at Chongjin for several days at a time.

The talk of stealing lignite made Yeong-dae think about his mother. She had stolen from the food storehouse to keep him and his sister from starving. Yeong-dae wondered whom the food in the storehouse was for. Since the government kept talking about its military-first policy, it was probably for feeding soldiers. Yeong-dae had been taught that North Korea needed the army to hold off the South Korean and American foes. But if all the people starved to death, who could become a soldier? Even schools were closing because there wasn't enough to eat, and children were becoming *kkotjebi*. Who could become a soldier and pledge their loyalty to the country? It occurred to Yeong-dae that his mother might've been thinking this way when she stole from the storehouse.

When the next train carrying lignite chugged into Chongjin Station, the *kkotjebi* clambered aboard the train cars like acrobats. Since it was Yeong-dae's first time, he wasn't as agile as the others. The children who had stolen lignite several times before were as light on their feet as cats. After pulling back the cover on the train car, they busily filled the sacks they had brought with lignite. Suddenly Geun-bae whistled shrilly.

"Yeong-dae! Get down quickly!" Nam-sik yelled.

With his hands trembling, Yeong-dae tied his sack of lignite. Someone was blowing a whistle close by. Geun-bae and Nam-sik yelled at Yeong-dae as they ran, pulling their sacks of lignite behind them.

"Yeong-dae! Throw down the sack first and then jump down fast!"

Yeong-dae dragged the heavy sack to the side and pushed it off the car. Just at that moment, the train began to move with a clatter. Yeong-dae was gripped by the fear that he wouldn't be able to get down. From far away, Nam-sik and Geun-bae were motioning for him to hurry and jump. Yeong-dae couldn't move a muscle, as if his feet were glued to the train car. The train gradually picked up speed. The train attendant was blowing his whistle, moving toward the car that Yeong-dae was on. It looked like Yeong-dae would be caught then and there. It was a dangerous moment. If he jumped, he might hit his head on the train tracks. Yeong-dae thought that he was about to die. Yeong-ok flashed before his eyes. He thought of his mother, who had also been caught stealing.

In desperation, Yeong-dae jumped as far as he could, and fell to the ground with a thud. Fortunately, there was a pile of dirt where he fell. He quickly got to his feet to run, but one of his ankles gave way under him. It looked like he'd sprained his ankle. Nam-sik ran over to him and slung Yeong-dae's arm over his shoulder. He dragged Yeong-dae off in such a hurry that Yeong-dae barely had time to think about the pain. For a long time, they could hear the whistle blowing angrily. Nam-sik didn't say anything until they'd gotten away from the station.

"You can't let yourself get that scared," he told Yeong-dae. "We all almost got caught because of you!"

Yeong-dae massaged his ankle. His heart was still pounding, even then.

"You didn't bring the sack of lignite either, did you?" Nam-sik asked. "I saw another kid who hesitated like you did. His leg got caught under the train, and he became a cripple. You have to be careful from now on."

"I understand, Nam-sik," Yeong-dae said. "I'm sorry."

When Yeong-dae was younger, he trusted the Great Leader and the Dear Leader more than he did his own mother and father. But now, the Great Leader and the Dear Leader were of no use to him. Now, the only thing that he could trust was mud-splattered noodles that had fallen on the street and corn kernels that people had stepped on. Only food—precious food—could keep Yeong-ok alive.

I'm Sorry, Yeong-ok

Once it was winter, Yeong-ok's belly started to swell to an unnatural size. Sometimes, she coughed all night long. Yeong-dae didn't understand why her stomach kept getting bigger, blowing up like a balloon, when the rest of her was so frail that it looked as if a gust of wind could've blown her away. Her face started to turn yellow, and the rims of her eyes became yellow as well.

Nam-sik said Yeong-ok had "malli"—short for malnutrition. People throughout North Korea were suffering and dying from this condition, and it went without saying that *kkotjebi* dealt with it, too.

When the temperature dropped below freezing, the *kkotjebi*

curled up next to chimneys and crawled into little sheds to get some sleep. Song-hwa got frostbite on her toes and couldn't walk anymore. Yeong-dae found a spot next to a chimney where Yeong-ok and Song-hwa could sleep. Geun-bae brought some old tattered clothing and spread it out on the ground. Later, Yeong-dae learned that the clothing had been taken off a corpse. When they needed some clothes to wrap themselves up in, *kkotjebi* couldn't afford to be picky.

Yeong-dae wasn't very happy about taking clothing from dead bodies, but the others didn't seem too bothered by it. It was the only way they could keep themselves from freezing to death.

Yeong-dae rustled up some old sheets and hung them up like a tent to keep out the rain and snow. Nam-sik and Geun-bae sifted through the trash and brought back anything that could keep away the cold, covering the ground with a thick layer of rags.

On very cold nights, the *kkotjebi* heated water. Since they didn't have a heater, the next best way to stay warm was a plastic bottle filled with hot water. Plastic bottles were essential for helping *kkotjebi* survive the winter.

Slowly, the color faded from Yeong-ok's face. On some days,

she could barely even open her eyes and drifted back to sleep. Afraid that she'd freeze to death, Yeong-dae would fill two plastic bottles with hot water and place the first one, and then the other, between her little arms each time he woke up. When she wasn't moving, he'd put his ear up to her mouth and listen for breathing sounds. He couldn't relax until he was sure she was still breathing.

Even when Yeong-dae went out to beg or forage for food, he'd find himself filled with dread. Terrified that something had happened to Yeong-ok, he would dash back to check on her.

One time when Yeong-ok woke up, she opened her eyes, parted her lips, and muttered in a voice so low that Yeong-dae could barely hear it.

"Yeong-dae," Yeong-ok said, "I want to eat some of that *kkojangtteok* that Mom makes," she said.

Yeong-ok hadn't asked for *injeolmi*, a rice cake covered with savory bean power, or *sirutteok*, another type of rice cake made by stuffing red bean crumbs between layers. She'd asked for *kkojangtteok*, which was little more than corn flour mashed up with water and steamed. Yeong-dae got so choked up when he heard this that he was unable to answer.

As Yeong-ok's belly swelled, it became harder and harder for her to breathe. It helped a little if Yeong-dae lay on his side and held her. Now, he couldn't leave his sister's side even for a moment. Nam-sik and Geun-bae shook their heads with concern when they looked at Yeong-ok. They didn't think that she'd get better.

One day when Geun-bae was picking up kindling for their fire, he ran over to Yeong-dae.

"Yeong-dae, hurry and cover up Yeong-ok!" he whispered. "If they catch sight of her, they might load her up and carry her off while she's still alive!"

Startled by Geun-bae's words, Yeong-dae quickly lay down in front of Yeong-ok to hide her.

"Geun-bae, who are 'they'?"

Before Geun-bae could answer, a couple of soldiers entered the alley. They were pushing a wheelbarrow and rummaging around. In the wheelbarrow were a few big sacks containing some bulky objects. For some reason, Yeong-dae felt a chill.

"What's in the sacks in the wheelbarrow, Geun-bae?" Yeong-dae asked.

"Hush!" Geun-bae said in a low voice. "Those soldiers are carting off people from the market who've starved or frozen to death. I've heard that they bury all the dead bodies in one big pile. When you die, they treat you like a wild animal. That's why you have to cling to life with everything you've got. Don't you ever forget that!"

Geun-bae said there were several frozen *kkotjebi* and old beggars in the wheelbarrow. He told Yeong-dae not to let the soldiers see Yeong-ok.

"They say the soldiers can tell if a person is going to live or die just by looking at them," Geun-bae went on. "If they think someone's going to die, they put them in the wagon even if they're still breathing. A little while ago, I heard there was even one kid who came to in the pile of dead bodies and managed to crawl out."

Hearing that, Yeong-dae's face went as white as a sheet. He pushed Yeong-ok further inside the shelter and made sure she was well hidden.

That night, Yeong-ok spoke to Yeong-dae drowsily, her eyes shut.

"Yeong-dae, I want to eat fried grasshoppers."

He thought his heart might break.

"Yeong-ok, it's winter right now," he told her. "Next fall, I'll catch a grasshopper and fry it up for you."

Yeong-dae wasn't sure whether she'd heard him or not, but her eyelids fluttered and a faint smile played across her face.

"Yeong-dae, where's Mom? I bet it's not cold where she's living, huh?"

There was something weird about Yeong-ok that day. What in the world could she be thinking? Didn't she know that Mom was locked up in the internment camp? Yeong-dae suddenly missed his mother with every fiber of his being. Was she still at the camp? They said she'd never be let out, so he guessed she probably was. Yeong-ok might be on the verge of death. He felt so sad that neither his mother nor older sister were there with them. Yeong-ok was murmuring again, her lips barely open.

"Yeong-dae, Yeong-ran did a bad thing. She left us so she could eat rice all by herself. Yeong-dae, I want to go see Yeong-ran so I can eat rice, too. Didn't Yeong-ran say she ate white rice every day? Ah, there's a hot bowl of rice over there. Look at the steam! Let's hurry over there, Yeong-dae. Wow! It's rice."

Yeong-ok had hardly ever talked about their older sister, and he was surprised that Yeong-ok would mention her. She was making less and less sense. When Yeong-dae put his hand on his little sister's forehead, he was shocked to find how hot it was. She had a raging fever.

"Yeong-ok, it hurts a lot, doesn't it? Yeong-ok, you can't die."

"I want to go see Mom. Mom said she'd cook me some *kkojangtteok*. Mom . . . Mom," she moaned.

Yeong-ok was crying, and the expression on her face showed that she was in pain.

"Yeong-dae, I think I got sick because I didn't eat this. I was saving this to give to you," she said.

She handed Yeong-dae a used tube of toothpaste. Nearly all of the toothpaste had been squeezed out. *Kkotjebi* thought of toothpaste as a miracle cure for stomach ailments. The scraps of food that they found in the market were usually covered with dirt or came from a pile of trash. Sometimes, the food gave them stomachaches and diarrhea. No one knew who came up with the idea first, but *kkotjebi* started eating a little toothpaste from time to time, believing it would prevent food poisoning. They thought that if they had a little toothpaste after eating, it would sterilize the dirty food. Yeong-dae had his doubts about whether this really worked, but decided to believe it. That was the only thing that could give him peace of mind about what he had to eat.

Because Yeong-dae was always worried about his sickly sister, he'd given her a used tube of toothpaste he found instead of keeping it for himself. Yeong-ok had treasured the tube, it seemed, hardly eating any of it.

Yeong-dae gripped the tube that his sister had given him in his fist. Tears dripped to the ground. Outside the shelter, snow flurries were falling.

Yeong-ok's body was burning up, but she shivered with the cold. Since the chimney had lost its heat by now, Yeong-dae pulled her close and wrapped his body around hers. Yeong-ok's breath started coming out in little gasps. Yeong-dae held her hands tightly in his own. Her hands had been hot with fever, but were now cooling. Yeong-dae relaxed a little. It seemed like her fever was dying down.

At some point, Yeong-dae realized that he no longer heard the sound of Yeong-ok breathing. He pressed his face against her mouth, and sure enough, no breath was coming out. He'd thought her fever was passing, but her body was cooling because her heart had stopped. Yeong-dae held his sister in his arms and tried to hold back his sobs. His weeping woke up Geun-bae and Nam-sik.

"Nam-sik, Yeong-ok stopped breathing! Oh, Yeong-ok, Yeong-ok. . ."

Yeong-dae felt like his heart was being torn to pieces.

"Nam-sik," Yeong-dae said through his tears. "She told me she wanted to eat fried grasshoppers. She told me she wanted to eat *kkojangtteok*. . ."

Nam-sik got a small fire going.

"They say the soldiers who collect bodies throw them all in a big pit and bury them together," he said. "I'd feel terrible if that happened to Yeong-ok."

Yeong-dae shook his head, his whole body trembling.

"No! I'm going to bury her. At least I can do that for her."

Yeong-dae just couldn't give Yeong-ok to the soldiers.

In the morning, black lice came crawling off of Yeong-ok's body. Yeong-dae felt goose bumps all over his body. He'd heard that lice leave dead bodies as they cool. He felt like his sister had died because these filthy insects had eaten her skin and drank her blood. He felt like the lice had murdered his sister. He flung the lice-infested rags to the floor and stomped on them savagely.

"Look at the bloated bellies of these filthy lice!" Yeong-dae screamed. "They stuffed their bellies sucking Yeong-ok's blood. Yeong-ok died because of these stupid lice. I'm going to kill all of them! The Great Leader and the Dear Leader are both good for nothing. They're all good for nothing. People say they're the sun shining down on us, but they're not. They're worthless."

In a frenzy, Yeong-dae stamped his feet on the ground, trying to crush the lice. His older sister had run away from home, his father had died, his mom had been taken away, and Yeong-ok was dead, too. Now, Yeong-dae was completely on his own. He didn't want to live on his own. He kept pounding the ground with his feet until he fell over with exhaustion. Nam-sik helped Yeong-dae back to his feet.

"What's the matter with you?" said Nam-sik. "Yeong-dae, cut it out!"

"Let go of me! Let me go! I hate them all. I'm going to kill them all!"

Nam-sik slapped Yeong-dae across the face.

"Listen to me, Yeong-dae! What's gotten into you?"

"Let go of me, I said! It's all pointless."

Nam-sik held on to Yeong-dae as firmly as he could. Yeong-dae thrashed, trying to get out of Nam-sik's grip, but Nam-sik was stronger, and he didn't let go. After sobbing for a long time, Yeong-dae's head gradually began to clear. What should he do with his life now? Should he end it all and follow Yeong-ok? He stared down at Yeong-ok's tiny body, which was slowly getting colder.

Just then, he saw soldiers tossing more frozen bodies into the cart the way they might pick up trash. Yeong-dae hurried to cover his sister's body with some old clothing, afraid that the soldiers might notice her. After that, he kept watching his sister's body, not leaving her side.

Yeong-dae spent two days next to Yeong-ok, as if he were dead, too.

"There's nothing you can do for her," Geun-bae said as he sat next to Yeong-dae. "Keep this up, and you'll freeze to death, too. Just let the soldiers have her."

"I can't do that," Yeong-dae said firmly. "Would you if you were in my place? This is my little sister we're talking about. She's the only one I have!"

"How long are you going to leave her like this?" Nam-sik asked, helping Geun-bae in the attempt to persuade Yeong-dae. "The ground is frozen solid. How can we hope to bury her? If the ground weren't frozen, we could try something, but there's nothing we can do. Just let her go."

Yeong-dae jumped to his feet.

"Nam-sik, you've got to help me. I'm going to look for a place to bury Yeong-ok."

"All right, let's see what we can find," Nam-sik said as he

stood up. "Let's see if there's somewhere we can bury her."

With some reluctance, Geun-bae got up, too, and the three boys left the market area. They plodded through fields covered in snow and went into the hills beyond. But the snow was piled up even higher in the hills, and there was no way they could bury Yeong-ok there. Even if there hadn't been any snow, they had no tools to dig a grave in the frozen ground.

Yeong-dae and his two friends trudged back to their shelter. Geun-bae's sister Song-hwa was right where they'd left her, but Yeong-ok's body was nowhere to be seen. Yeong-dae ran around the area, desperately trying to find her.

He tried asking Song-hwa what had happened, but she just kept shaking her head. He'd never been more frustrated that Song-hwa was mute.

Nam-sik and Geun-bae shook their heads and gazed up at the sky.

"Hell, we might freeze to death one of these days, too," Nam-sik said, trying to console Yeong-dae. "Who do you think is next? Why is the world so messed up? We could all die just like Yeong-ok before spring gets here."

Geun-bae picked up the thread when Nam-sik was finished.

"Yeong-dae, what can we do, as weak as we are? We don't

have a choice. This is a dog's life, you know."

But the two boys' words went in one of Yeong-dae's ears and right out the other.

"I feel so bad for Yeong-ok," he said. "I don't know why we have to keep living like this. I really don't know."

As Yeong-dae sobbed, Nam-sik, Geun-bae, and Song-hwa started crying quietly too. Yeong-dae wandered around the area, trying to find where the soldiers dumped the dead bodies, but there was no way to tell because everything was covered in snow.

Yeong-dae didn't want to do anything. He wasn't hungry, and he didn't even want to live. Finally, Nam-sik forced Yeong-dae to his feet, grabbed his hand, and started pulling him along behind him.

"Yeong-dae, hurry and come along. If you keep acting like this, you'll die, too."

Yeong-dae followed Nam-sik and went to the market. Women were melting snow and selling hot water. Only five won to rinse your face with water, they called, and ten won for a wash with soap. They must've sold all of their home furnishings—down to the spoons and chopsticks—and had nothing left to sell, Yeong-dae thought. Why else would they be forced to sell hot water for washing? The women selling the water shouted at passersby to take a moment to wash their faces. But the women's own faces were as black as soot. They seemed to be so busy selling water that they didn't have time to clean themselves up.

Yeong-dae was sorry that he hadn't been able to wash Yeong-ok's face one last time.

When he was younger, he'd memorized every single fact about the childhood of the Great Leader and the Dear Leader. Each day, he would bow his head before their portraits. The Great Leader, he was told, was like a bright sun for all Koreans. He was told that the Great Leader had made the world's best country to live in. But now, all of that seemed like just a dream. The life that Yeong-dae now led each day at the market was filled with darkness. There was no moonlight or even starlight there, let alone sunlight.

Time was the medicine that cured Yeong-dae's heartache. As he walked around the market each day, he was too preoccupied with filling his empty belly to have much time to think about Yeong-ok, or even feel sad about her.

On to Musan

The *kkotjebi* started sleeping beneath the bridge again sometime before the frozen water began to thaw.

Geun-bae spread out some old clothing beside a road frequented by many people and had Song-hwa sit there. His sister would hold out her empty hands toward people passing by, asking them for something to eat.

One day, Yeong-dae was hanging around the noodle restaurant with Nam-sik and Geun-bae, waiting for customers to leave some food behind. Maybe a week had gone by since Song-hwa started begging by the road. All of a sudden, they saw something strange happening down the road where she was begging.

A couple of suspicious-looking men were standing near Song-hwa, one of whom laid a hand on the girl. Song-hwa was struggling, trying to get out of his grip, and bellowing in an eerie, grating voice. Since she was mute, her voice sounded like the screech of a wild animal. Geun-bae took off toward his sister, and Yeong-dae and Nam-sik dashed after him. Geun-bae charged the man grabbing Song-hwa and head-butted him in the belly.

"You'd better let go of her hand, Mister!" Geun-bae shouted.

The man who had grabbed Song-hwa was bowled over by Geun-bae's unexpected charge. Song-hwa let out a weird shriek and scurried behind her brother to hide. In a split second, the market was filled with pandemonium.

"These are men who kidnap women and sell them!" Nam-sik shouted to the people around them. "You've got to report them!"

Frightened by Nam-sik's words, the men made a getaway.

Yeong-dae's blood ran cold when he heard the talk about selling women.

"Nam-sik, what was that about selling women?"

"You mean you don't know?" Nam-sik replied. "I'm talking about merchants who take women and sell them to men in

China."

Yeong-dae had a hard time understanding what selling a person might mean.

"They sell people in China?" he asked, confused.

"These people convince women that they'll get them jobs, and then they sell them to single Chinese men in farming towns," Geun-bae said, his clenched fists still trembling with rage. "That was a very close call for Song-hwa. I didn't know that the kidnappers were also trying to put their paws on little girls now. They're as bad as animals! Terrible people who sell other people so they can fill their own bellies."

Yeong-dae was suddenly reminded of his older sister, Yeong-ran. He asked Nam-sik if that could've happened to her.

"It's possible," Nam-sik said. "Those creeps con women, telling them that they'll keep them well-fed and get them work if they go to China. But what they really do is sell them to old bachelors or widowers in Chinese farming villages. The way I see it, your sister could've been sold in China as well. I've heard lots of stories like that."

Yeong-dae had heard something similar from his aunt, but at the time, he hadn't paid it any mind. He'd believed that nothing of the sort could've happened to his sister.

But now that Nam-sik was saying the same thing, he felt that his sister must've been sold in China as well. If she had found work, why hadn't they heard from her, not even once? It was more likely that she hadn't sent her family any money or contacted them because she'd been sold to a Chinese farmer. Yeong-dae wanted to find his older sister so badly, whatever it took.

"Nam-sik, where do you think my sister was sold to?" he said, clenching his fists. "What can I do to figure out where my sister went?"

Nam-sik just shook his head.

"How would you find out where she went?" he said. "The country of China is as big as the sky above us. To find your sister, you'd have to cross the river into China. But you don't speak Chinese, so how can you find her?" Nam-sik paused, and then went on. "Besides, if you get caught, you'll be punished for crossing the river. They'll say you betrayed the fatherland. Haven't you heard that if you get thrown in prison, you could die there?"

"Nam-sik, I've got to find my sister. I'm going to cross the river," Yeong-dae said.

"If you're going to cross, make sure you do your homework

first," Geun-bae said worriedly. "You'll have to make a lot of preparations as well."

From that day on, the only thing Yeong-dae thought about was how to find his older sister. He even opened up the notebook that she'd bought him. He hadn't written in it for some time.

Yeong-ran, wait for me. I'm going to find you!

After he wrote the vow in his notebook, his heart overflowed with emotions. If he was going to cross the river to find his sister, he'd have to learn about China. He started paying closer attention to Joseonjok merchants, whom he'd always ignored before. While taking care of Yeong-ok, he'd never had any time to worry about anything else, but now, he dedicated himself to getting ready to go looking for his older sister. He also needed a plan for crossing the river. Just the thought of it filled him with energy.

"Yeong-dae, first things first. You need to take better care of your body," Nam-sik told him. "You'll need some real grit to go begging in a foreign country."

Geun-bae had some advice for him, too.

"You shouldn't go until you're completely ready, but don't wait too long, either," he said. "You have to cross the river while the water is still frozen, before it thaws."

After Yeong-dae heard what Nam-sik and Geun-bae had to say, he realized that he needed to hurry. But before he left North Korea, he wanted to visit his home and his grandmother's house again. What had happened to his mother? His neighbor might've even heard some news about his older sister.

"In Musan, it's easy to cross the river," Geun-bae said. "Musan is close to here, so you can head there if you're planning on crossing the river. I hope you find your sister, too."

Nam-sik suddenly jumped into the conversation as if he'd been holding something back.

"I'm going to Musan, too. If I go, that'll mean two less mouths to feed here."

Geun-bae's eyes popped when he heard that.

"Nam-sik! You're going, too?" he asked.

Nam-sik nodded his head tiredly.

"We don't have any hope here, you know," he said. "I want to eat rice, too."

"I'd go with you if Song-hwa was in good health. If I get a chance later, I'll go after you. You two go ahead and wait for me!"

Yeong-dae was tremendously happy to hear that Nam-sik would be going with him. Yeong-dae decided that he should go to his parents' house one more time. How he hoped that his mother had been let out of prison! If nothing else, he figured that he could find out what had happened to her. He thought that his older sister surely must have sent a message while he'd been away.

"Nam-sik, wait for me here just a few days," Yeong-dae said. "I've got to visit Kilju. I'll come back as quickly as I can."

"You're going back home?" Nam-sik asked uncertainly. "You have to hurry back. If the ice breaks, it won't be easy to cross the river!"

Yeong-dae left for Kilju the very next day. When he arrived at his old village, his house looked as desolate as ever.

As soon as he got there, he went to find Mrs. Kim. When she saw him, she shook her head.

"Yeong-dae, your mother—," she said, and broke off with a heavy sigh. "How can I tell you this?'

"Mrs. Kim, what happened to Mom? Did they let her go?"

The woman shook her head.

"They say your mother had an accident at the internment camp."

"What, an accident? What happened? Did they take her out of the camp and put her in a hospital?"

Mrs. Kim slowly shook her head before answering.

"If only that had happened! Your mother isn't with us anymore. I'm trying to tell you that she had a really serious accident."

Yeong-dae's legs seemed to go limp. He'd thought that he could meet his mother again, someday. But now she'd gone to a place where they could never meet again. It was only a short time ago that he had had to say goodbye to Yeong-ok. He couldn't believe this was happening. He tried to keep control of his feelings.

"Where did they bury Mom?" he asked Mrs. Kim, after a long pause. "I'd like to go see her grave, at least."

But the woman just shook her head, not saying a word. For some time, Yeong-dae just cried. He wasn't able to say anything.

"Mrs. Kim," he finally managed to say. "Have you by any chance heard anything from my sister?"

The woman shook her head once more.

"If my sister comes here," Yeong-dae said, "can you tell her that I crossed the river to go looking for her?"

"You're going across the river?" she asked with surprise.

Yeong-dae nodded his head quietly. Now, Yeong-ran was the only other person in Yeong-dae's family who was still alive. He had to find her, and do so quickly. He also realized that there was no time to stop by his grandmother's old house. Instead, he headed straight back to Sunam Market.

The day after he returned, Yeong-dae and Nam-sik started paying careful attention to the Joseonjok merchants. Though they were Korean by blood, their faces and the way they dressed set them apart from North Koreans. Joseonjok faces were fleshy and full of color, and their clothing was of much better quality than what North Koreans wore.

Yeong-dae and Nam-sik started going up to female Joseonjok traders who looked kind and asking if they could carry their goods or run errands for them. At first, the women shooed the boys away, assuming that they were going to run off with their goods as soon as they got their hands on them. But the women started opening up to the boys when they realized that they were serious about helping them.

The Joseonjok merchants generally brought food from China and sold it in North Korea, and then took seafood or minerals from North Korea back to China. Yeong-dae followed the women around and became an errand boy for them.

After five days of this, a Joseonjok woman left Chongjin for Musan, carrying products from the sea with her. When the woman boarded a train bound for Musan, Yeong-dae and Nam-sik were right beside her.

Musan wasn't that far from Chongjin, but because of trouble with electricity, their train didn't reach Musan Station until three days later. The merchant praised them for the good work they'd done and put a few coins in their hands before they parted ways.

Musan was right next to the Chinese border, and it was vibrant and full of energy. In the market, it seemed like there were even more Joseonjok traders than North Korean traders. A lot of iron was in the mines around Musan, and Yeong-dae saw a factory that was running, with smoke coming out of the chimney. He hadn't seen that for a while.

It even seemed like the *kkotjebi* had a little more skin on their bones here. Yeong-dae and Nam-sik had heard stories about how the *kkotjebi* in Musan would sneak across the Tumen River to beg for a bowl of rice at the homes of Joseonjok before crossing back into North Korea. Yeong-dae wasn't sure whether he really believed that, but the thought of rice made his heart turn a somersault.

The boys also heard that there were even *kkotjebi* who would cross the river and beg in front of Chinese hotels. The guests at these hotels were usually South Korean tourists, it seemed. The *kkotjebi* said it wasn't hard to beg some money out of these tourists.

"Nam-sik, is South Korea really a wealthy country?" Yeong-dae asked his older friend. "It's hard to believe that poor South Koreans just hand out money like that. I'm not sure what to think about these stories of *kkotjebi* going back and forth across the river, either. What happens if they get caught by the border guards while they're trying to cross the river?"

"You can't believe all of these stories, but they're not as crazy as you might think," Nam-sik said, to Yeong-dae's surprise. "I've heard a lot of stories while begging in the market. I've known that South Korea was a rich country for a long time now. Well, we need to start putting our plan into action."

Not only had Nam-sik been a *kkotjebi* longer than Yeong-dae, but he was older, too. This meant that he knew quite a bit, and could quickly learn things that he didn't know. Yeong-dae helped Nam-sik gather together some dried corn kernels to use as an emergency food supply.

The two boys walked along the river banks, looking for the safest place to cross the river. But while they explored, they took care to pick up scrap paper and metal as well to avoid arousing suspicion from the border guards. At night, they slept in the hills, and by day, they took note of the locations of the guard posts as they scrounged for scraps.

Three days later, they settled on the perfect place for crossing the river. The spot wasn't very far from a guard post, but because it was at the bottom of a steep slope that jutted out into the river, there was no sentry station there. Not only that, but if they were spotted, it would only take a few minutes to scurry back up the hill and into the woods. Best of all, the crossing point wasn't directly visible from the guard post.

After making up their minds about where they would cross, they hid in the woods atop the hill and watched to see how many guards were stationed at the post. They also observed when the guards changed and how many times each patrol made its rounds. But the most important thing was how much time passed between one patrol and the next. They had to cross the river in the time it took for one patrol to pass and the next to arrive.

The Night Crossing

The river was still frozen all the way to the bottom. Just the previous night, Yeong-dae and Nam-sik had been about to attempt the crossing when the border guards caught someone else trying to do the same thing a little further down the river. The two boys had been forced to delay their plans a whole day. But today, they had to make it to the other side — or else.

The sun dipped below the horizon, and the darkness slowly began to spread. The hair on Yeong-dae's head was standing on end.

"Until it's completely dark, let's have a few dried corn kernels to take the edge off our hunger," Nam-sik said as he opened up the backpack.

"You bet!" Yeong-dae said. He popped some kernels into his mouth and started munching on them.

Yeong-dae was so tense that even the sound of his chewing sounded unusually loud to him. He fixed his eyes on the lights at the guard station in the distance just like the day before, waiting for the changing of the guard.

Finally, it was the moment they'd been waiting for.

"This is it! We're going now!" Nam-sik said, starting forward.

They raced down the steep slope once again. Soon they reached the edge of the frozen river.

The moment Yeong-dae's feet touched the ice, his entire body tensed up even more than before. He felt like someone was grabbing him by the scruff of the neck. He paused, staying as quiet as he could, afraid that a bullet would come zinging out of the darkness at him.

"Run!"

Nam-sik dashed forward as quick as a bolt of lightning, and Yeong-dae sprinted after him as fast as he could. Suddenly, flashlight beams flickered around them.

"Run with everything you've got!" Nam-sik shouted desperately.

Yeong-dae pumped his legs and ran. He felt like he was flying through the air. The flashlight beams lit up the ice beneath his feet. Whistles were shrieking all around him. From somewhere behind them, one of the border guards was bellowing at them to stop.

Yeong-dae ran with everything he had, just as Nam-sik told him. After a short time, he heard the crackle of ice under his feet. It was the sound that frozen grass makes when it crunches under your shoes in the winter. This meant that they had reached the gravel-covered bank of the river.

"Hurry! This way!"

Nam-sik's urgent voice came to him from out there, ahead in the darkness. Panting with fatigue, Yeong-dae lurched toward the sound. All of a sudden, he lost his footing and went sprawling. When he tried to get back on his feet, a spasm of pain shot through his left ankle. Not again!

"What's the matter?" Nam-sik yelled, impatience in his voice. "Hurry up and run this way!"

"Nam-sik, my ankle . . .!" Yeong-dae said, moaning. He must have sprained his ankle again when he fell.

Yeong-dae could hear the tinkle of ice breaking again. Nam-sik must be coming back for him.

"Oh, great. Not again!" Nam-sik said when he came running

back. "If the Chinese soldiers catch us, we're done for. Here, lean on my shoulder. Come on!"

Yeong-dae clung to Nam-sik's shoulder and hurried along, putting as much weight as he could on his good right foot. They kept running, little knowing whether they were moving along a road, through a field, or in the hills. Dark trees loomed in front of them like terrible creatures, blocking their path. Sweat slid down Yeong-dae's spine. Each time his left foot touched the ground, a bolt of pain seemed to shoot through his entire body. It was only when they reached the woods that Nam-sik came to a halt.

"All right," he said. "Let's take a little break."

Yeong-dae wasn't sure how far they'd run, but his ankle was in agony and his heart felt like it was about to explode. Across the river, flashlight beams swept rapidly in all directions. Yeong-dae could hardly believe that they'd made it across the river.

"Nam-sik, have we really crossed the river?"

"You bet! This is China. We very nearly got caught."

"The border guards started yelling when they saw us, didn't they?"

"I heard that once someone crosses the river and sets foot

in China, the North Korean border guards can't shoot at them," Nam-sik said, relaxing a little and breathing a sigh of relief. "That's the law, I guess. You can't shoot a gun at another country. When the guards saw what we were doing, we'd already made it to China. Hey, let me see your hurt ankle."

Yeong-dae had sprained the ankle when they were stealing lignite from the train at Chongjin Station, and now it was acting up again. Nam-sik grabbed hold of Yeong-dae's left foot and yanked it toward him. Yeong-dae very nearly let out a shriek.

"You didn't break it, did you?" Nam-sik said, with worry in his voice. "This is the ankle that you sprained before, isn't it? Keep massaging it. What are we going to do if you can't walk?"

Nam-sik kept pulling the foot forward, his hands firm. Yeong-dae started sweating as he massaged the ankle, trying to endure the pain.

"Do you think you can walk? Try putting a little weight on your foot," Nam-sik said.

The older boy helped Yeong-dae to his feet. Yeong-dae gingerly tried walking on his left foot. It felt a little better. But the sweat had cooled while he was rubbing his ankle, and now he felt cold. He trembled like a leaf.

"Let's rest here for a little and then move on early in the morning," Nam-sik suggested. "We can't see anything. We can't even tell the road from the woods. Anyway, keep rubbing your body. You have to get some heat into your body."

Just like Nam-sik said, Yeong-dae kept rubbing his arms and legs. In his head, he whispered to his sister.

Yeong-ran! I've set foot in China now, too! You only have to wait for me a little longer.

Yeong-dae was excited with the hope that he'd see his sister soon. A faint light began to fill the eastern sky. Nam-sik helped Yeong-dae stand up.

"OK," the older boy said. "It's time to move now."

The two headed in the direction of a large road they could see. Worried that they might get caught by the Chinese police if they moved on the main road, they stayed in the woods on the side of the road.

Yeong-dae's left ankle gradually began to hurt more and more. Now and again, a woodland creature would appear and then scurry off, startled by the boys' footsteps. The wild woods went on and on, with no apparent end. They'd walked so long that Yeong-dae felt an intense desire to lie down where he was and just go to sleep.

"Nam-sik, I can't walk any further," Yeong-dae said. "Can we take a little break?"

Nam-sik must have felt the same way, because he quickly snapped off some pine branches from a nearby tree, laid them on the ground, and had Yeong-dae sit on them.

"I'm sorry, Nam-sik."

"You don't need to say that. Hurry up and massage your body."

Nam-sik scooped up some snow and took a bite before handing Yeong-dae some to eat, too. But snow couldn't satisfy Yeong-dae's hunger.

"Nam-sik, I need to eat something," he said. "I'm so hungry, I could eat a horse."

"All right. We can eat some kernels of corn at least. We skipped lunch anyway."

Nam-sik pulled the corn kernels out of the backpack and handed some to Yeong-dae. Once he had some food in his belly, he felt like they might just make it. His throat was a little dry, so he took a bite of snow. No matter how hard Yeong-dae looked, he couldn't see any signs that people lived in the area. This confused him.

"The *kkotjebi* said that when you crossed the river, there'd be a hotel and you could eat rice. So where exactly are we right now?"

"First of all, we have to go somewhere people live," Nam-sik told him. "Here, we're still in the middle of the woods. If we follow that road, though, it'll take us to a village."

"How do you know?"

"If there's a road, there must be people who use it, and if there are people around, you know there must be a village nearby," Nam-sik explained. "Let's rest for a little while and then get going again."

Eating some corn had helped Yeong-dae stave off the worst of his hunger, and he felt like he'd gotten some of his energy back. Both boys got up again and walked alongside the road. They couldn't think of a better plan. They walked and walked until Yeong-dae seemed to lose all feeling in his body.

After continuing for quite some time, they saw some houses up ahead, near the main road. Yeong-dae was overjoyed.

"Nam-sik, houses! I see some houses over there!"

"It looks like this is where the village starts. Let's move faster now."

When he heard Nam-sik talk about a village, Yeong-dae felt his strength returning. First, they used the trees to conceal their movements as they moved closer to the village. Since they'd been walking all day, the sun had sunk far into the west.

After climbing a rise that overlooked the village, they studied the houses, trying to decide which one to approach. Judging by the smoke drifting up from the chimneys, the families in the village must be preparing dinner.

After watching the village for a while, Nam-sik turned to Yeong-dae with a grave expression on his face.

"Yeong-dae, listen up," he said. "Do you see the house that's closest to us? That one there, right by the edge of the woods? You stay here, and don't move. If we both go and both get caught, all of this effort was for nothing. I'm going to go ahead and scout out the situation. If everything's OK, I'll come back and get you. If I don't come back, just assume that something went wrong. If I don't return by tonight, go on and get out of here. Do you understand?"

This talk scared Yeong-dae, and he shook his head furiously.

"No, Nam-sik, let's just go together. I'm scared. What am I supposed to do by myself?"

"It's more dangerous if both of us go," Nam-sik said firmly, his jaw set. "Just do as I said."

Yeong-dae was afraid of being left by himself. Still, Nam-sik was right. If they went together, they could both get caught by the Chinese police.

Nam-sik slung the backpack onto his shoulders, got to his feet, and started walking cautiously toward the village. Hiding behind a tree, Yeong-dae watched Nam-sik go with eyes open wide.

Nam-sik slipped down toward the house on the edge of the woods as stealthily as a cat on the prowl. On his way down, he must have seen someone, as he suddenly dropped to all fours on the embankment between two fields and stayed perfectly still for some time before moving again. Yeong-dae's heart was racing.

Little by little, the village was disappearing into the darkness. Nam-sik's figure grew fainter and fainter until Yeong-dae couldn't see him any longer. Yeong-dae stayed quiet, hoping that nothing bad would happen to his friend.

Before long, lights began to flicker on in the village in one house after another. At last, a light began to twinkle in the window of the house that Nam-sik had been heading to. Yeong-dae was afraid that Nam-sik might not return. He resisted the urge to follow in Nam-sik's footsteps that very moment.

It wasn't easy for Yeong-dae to tell how long he'd waited. It could've been a few minutes—or a few days. He continued to wait, but Nam-sik didn't appear. What could've happened to him? Did the house he'd gone to belong to the Chinese police? What in the world should he do?

Yeong-dae felt like he'd been left all alone in a dark world. He couldn't put what Nam-sik had told him out of his head. If he didn't come back that night, Nam-sik said, Yeong-dae should head out on his own. Yeong-dae shook his head. He couldn't run away by himself like that.

After struggling to his feet, Yeong-dae started limping along toward the house where Nam-sik had gone. He couldn't imagine himself being separated from Nam-sik. Not only that, but since his leg hurt so badly, running away by himself wasn't really an option.

Carefully, Yeong-dae made his way closer to the house. He needed to find a place to hide so that he could figure out what was going on. When Yeong-dae had nearly reached the front of the house, he heard a man's voice.

"Be careful," the man said. "You must be sure not to let anyone see you."

"All right! I'll be right back," said a second person.

The second person, Yeong-dae realized at once, was Nam-sik. Yeong-dae was filled with relief. Nam-sik must've been on his way to get him. When Yeong-dae shuffled out of the shadows to let Nam-sik know he was there, the other boy jumped with surprise.

"Who—who are you?" he yelled.

"Nam-sik, it's me! Yeong-dae!"

Nam-sik seemed to be even more startled than Yeong-dae had been.

"Yeong-dae, why did you come here by yourself? That was risky!" he said. "I told you to stay put until I came to get you."

Nam-sik turned to the doorway, where an old man was standing. "Mr. Choi, this is my younger friend Yeong-dae. He came with me."

"Hurry on inside," the man said.

As soon as Yeong-dae entered the house, the old man wasted no time in shutting the door.

"No one saw you, did they?"

Yeong-dae assured him that no one had. Yeong-dae was shocked when he saw Nam-sik under the light. He'd washed his face and changed into neat clothes.

"Nam-sik, where did those clothes come from?"

"Mrs. Choi — the lady here, I mean — gave them to me," he said. "She said the clothes I was wearing stank!"

Nam-sik's new clothes were of better quality than anything Yeong-dae had ever worn in his life. The elderly couple and a boy who looked a little younger than Yeong-dae were staring at Yeong-dae. The old woman clucked her tongue.

"Welcome to our home. Not only is it cold out there, but you have a hurt ankle, by the looks of it," she said, eyeing him with concern. "My goodness! Just look at those rags you're wearing. Let's get you into some of our grandson's clothing."

After handing Yeong-dae a stack of new clothes, Mrs. Choi told him to wash up and get changed. Yeong-dae took the clothing that the woman had given him and then paused, turning to Nam-sik.

"Nam-sik, why were you so late?" he complained. "Do you have any idea how worried I was, waiting out there all by myself? I thought you'd gotten in trouble. I kept waiting, but you just didn't come."

"I wanted to go right away, but Mr. Choi said it was too dangerous. He told me to wait until it got dark."

"When you didn't come after hours and hours of waiting, I figured you'd been caught!"

"Huh?" Nam-sik said with surprise. "I was only gone for two hours."

"Two hours? I thought it'd been more like ten hours!"

While he was waiting by himself, time had passed so slowly that he could hardly stand it. But it seemed that only two hours had passed! Yeong-dae washed his face with the water the old woman had drawn for him and then changed into new clothing. He had no idea how long it had been since he had washed his face or worn proper clothing.

It was just then that the fragrance of rice started wafting through the house. Mrs. Choi was spooning out rice for Yeong-dae and Nam-sik to eat. Yeong-dae almost fainted at the savory aroma. He'd wanted to eat rice so badly! The old woman glanced at Yeong-dae as she carried a small folding table into the room.

"My word! Now that you've changed your clothing, you look like a completely different boy. Hurry up and eat your rice."

As soon as Yeong-dae saw the rice, he began salivating uncontrollably. It was a bowl of plain white rice without any corn, millet, mugwort, or other herbs mixed in. He'd never had such a luxury before.

"Dig in," Mrs. Choi encouraged him with a smile. "You're

lucky that you didn't freeze to death, Yeong-dae. To think that you were wearing this pile of rags in the middle of the winter! Go ahead and warm up your insides with this warm soup. It should help you thaw."

The woman stepped outside, carrying the tattered clothes that Yeong-dae had been wearing.

Yeong-dae wolfed down his food. Mouthfuls of white rice went down the hatch with barely time to chew them. When Mrs. Choi returned, she put another heaping scoop of rice in Yeong-dae's bowl.

"I just don't understand why North Korea keeps getting poorer and poorer," she said. "Just a few days ago, two women who'd crossed the river came by here. They were so thin that you could hardly tell if they were people or skeletons."

When Yeong-dae heard her mention women, he thought of his older sister. He wondered whether she'd passed by here after crossing the river.

The Elderly Acupuncturist

After Yeong-dae's muscles relaxed, his left ankle started to throb. Mr. Choi noticed him massaging his ankle and went to get a small box on the shelf.

"You said you sprained your ankle, didn't you? Let me take a look at it," the elderly man said, reaching for Yeong-dae's foot.

Yeong-dae was taken aback. He didn't understand why the old man wanted to look at his foot.

"Mr. Choi said he will put some needles in you," Nam-sik explained. "I told him all about your ankle."

Yeong-dae flinched at the word "needle." Nam-sik went on to say Mr. Choi was a highly regarded acupuncturist in the village.

The man examined Yeong-dae's left ankle, pressed firmly around the joint as he looked for the place to insert the needles. Each time he applied pressure, Yeong-dae's ankle throbbed. Trying to get his mind off the pain, Yeong-dae gazed around the room. The old couple didn't have a lot of furniture, but they did have a television.

Meanwhile, Mr. Choi was pulling the needles from the box.

"You need to be patient for a little while," he told Yeong-dae. "You'll get better soon after I put the needles in you. These needles are from South Korea. They're very good quality."

The word "South Korea" got Yeong-dae's attention.

Just then, the acupuncturist's wife turned on the TV.

"Darn it, I missed the beginning of the soap opera!" she said. "Take a look at that. That's Seoul."

Seoul? Yeong-dae wondered what country that was in.

"Mrs. Choi, where's Seoul?"

"What do you mean, where's Seoul? Seoul is Seoul, in the ROK."

"What? ROK? What's that?"

The old man and woman had a good laugh when they heard Yeong-dae's question.

"Huh, I guess you North Koreans probably refer to it as 'South

Korea,'" Mrs. Choi said. "'ROK' stands for the Republic of Korea. That's South Korea. Seoul is the capital of South Korea. Do you understand now?"

Yeong-dae's body tensed again when he heard that Seoul was the capital of South Korea. The television set showed a young man wearing a fancy suit walking along the banks of a river with a woman who was slimmer than his sister Yeong-ran. In the next scene, another young man — this one as good-looking as Chang-u — was walking into a huge building.

"You should study hard so that you can become as successful as that young man," the old woman said as she tousled her little grandson's hair. "If your mother and father earn a lot of money in South Korea, we'll be able to enjoy as good a life as anyone else has. Until that time, though, you have to study harder. That's how you can make your parents feel better."

Yeong-dae realized that the Joseonjok couple envied the lives of South Koreans. The image of South Korea he saw on the TV was the exact opposite of what he'd been taught in school. At first, it was so hard to believe that he thought the show was all a lie.

But they couldn't have faked the mountains and fields on the TV. And it wasn't just the fashionable clothes that the actors were wearing, either. The skyscrapers soaring up into the air and the cars zooming down the streets—they all looked incredible. North Korea had nothing that could even be compared to this.

Mr. Choi stuck six needles in Yeong-dae's ankle and told him to be patient for a little while. The needles stung a little when they entered his flesh, but after that, they didn't hurt anymore.

"Nam-sik," Yeong-dae told his friend in a low voice. "South Korea sure is something!"

"No kidding! I've heard about it before, but it's amazing to actually see what it's like."

"Nam-sik, what are we supposed to do now?"

First of all, we'll stay here tonight," the older boy said. "We can talk about our plans tomorrow. Mr. and Mrs. Choi are really great people. They're going to help us out."

Nam-sik didn't seem too worried about anything. After a while, Mr. Choi pulled the acupuncture needles from Yeong-dae's ankles and promised to give him another treatment the following morning. That night, Yeong-dae went to sleep thinking about the amazing view of South Korea he'd seen on TV.

After they ate breakfast the next morning, the old man

turned to Yeong-dae.

"Did you decide where you wanted to go before you came to China?" he asked. "Or did you just cross the river because you were hungry and wanted to get something to eat?"

Yeong-dae decided to tell Mr. Choi the truth.

"I came to find my sister," he said. "I think my sister was sold to a Chinese farmer. It's been more than three years since she left, and I still haven't heard anything from her."

"Putting people up for sale!" the old man said, his brows furrowing. "No matter where you live, there are always creeps like that. There was a young North Korean woman who got sold to a duck farm here in Helong. She even had a child, but now I guess she ran away."

Yeong-dae wondered whether the girl Mr. Choi mentioned might be Yeong-ran.

"She ran away?" he asked eagerly. "Where to?"

"Nine out of ten times, runaways get caught. They can't speak the language and don't know the way, so before long, they come to the attention of the Chinese police. Probably, she was taken back to North Korea."

It seemed to Yeong-dae that if he could just find out when the woman ran away, he could figure out whether it was Yeong-ran.

"When did she run away?"

"I don't know for sure, but it was probably two years ago," the man said.

"Mr. Choi, can I go to the duck farm?"

"What would you go there for? I'm telling you that she ran away. She's not there anymore."

"I mean that if I visit the farm and find out the details, I think I can figure out if it was my sister or not."

The old man shook his head grimly.

"The man who owns the duck farm isn't all there, if you know what I mean. Visiting the farm would be a waste of your time. He wouldn't give you the time of day. And, if he finds out that you're from North Korea, he might even report you to the police. There are a lot of Chinese who tell the police about people who've run away from North Korea in the hope of getting some money. You have to be careful."

"Mr. Choi, why did that North Korean woman run away?"

"Well, she was sold to a man against her will, and she was supposed to live with him even though he had some serious mental problems. From what I heard, he would lock her up and beat her for no good reason," the man said and sighed. "Takes your breath away, doesn't it?"

Yeong-dae wasn't ready to give up so easily, though.

"Mr. Choi, is there nowhere else where North Korean women live after they've been sold? Please, you have to help me find my sister!"

"I did hear that some kidnapped North Korean women are living in Wangqing, too," the old man said. "They say that when a country's in trouble, it's the little children and women who suffer first."

Yeong-dae wanted to meet the women who'd been kidnapped from North Korea, wherever they might be living.

"Where's Wangqing? How far do you have to go from here?" he asked.

"It takes about half a day by bus. But they won't be easy to find. Since it's against the law to pay for a North Korean woman to be brought here, these Chinese men hide them very carefully. And even if you do figure out where they are, it's not easy to meet them. Also, you have no way of knowing if it's your sister or not — until you see her."

"Mr. Choi, I have to find my sister! My whole family's dead now and she's all I have left," Yeong-dae pleaded as tears streamed from his eyes. "Please help me."

The old man was shaking his head. He said so many North Korean women had been abducted and sold in China. There was no way that Yeong-dae could meet them all.

"I just have to find my sister. . ."

Mr. Choi gazed at Yeong-dae's tear-filled eyes for some time and at last sighed.

"As it so happens, I'm going to Wangqing tomorrow to give someone acupuncture treatment," he said at last. "Wait here until I get back. You need some more acupuncture for your ankle, too. While I'm gone, you have to stay inside. Don't even stick your nose outside the door. The police could be nosing around at any time. I'll go to Wangqing and find out for you."

Yeong-dae felt immensely grateful to the old man.

"Mr. Choi, thank you so much!"

"It's not a big deal. North Korea is like this because it got saddled with the wrong leader. I feel bad for the people starving in North Korea. You wouldn't believe the lifestyle of people in South Korea. We're able to live as comfortably as we do because our son and his wife make money in South Korea and send some to us. I always feel bad that our grandson lives apart from his parents. That's why I couldn't just ignore you boys."

When the old man finished talking, his wife spoke up.

"A long time ago, North Korea had a much higher living standard than China. When we were young, we would cross the Tumen River when there wasn't anything to eat. In North Korea, we could get some rice and other food. When North Koreans cross the river, I think of those times. That's why I feed them their fill of hot rice."

Yeong-dae nodded his head to show he understood.

"Mr. Choi," he said, "I'd heard that South Korea was richer than the Republic before, but I was shocked by what I saw on TV."

"Sure! That's why our son went to South Korea to make some money, too. All of the young people who live in Joseonjok villages are obsessed with South Korea. And even in North Korea, knowledgeable people know the truth. That's why they're so determined to cross the river and go to South Korea. They say North Koreans who go to the South are given money for resettlement and even a house. That's why there are lots of people who'd rather take their chances in crossing the river than starve. Of course, not all of them make it."

When Mr. Choi finished talking, Nam-sik spoke up.

"Do North Koreans who go to the South really get money

and houses to help them settle there?"

"That's what they say. From what I hear, South Korea gives North Korean refugees apartments to live in — even though there are homeless people in South Korea. Supposedly, they get quite a bit of resettlement money, too. People take out a loan to go to South Korea and then pay back the loan with the resettlement money they're given."

Nam-sik's eyes were bright with interest.

"Mr. Choi, I'd like to go to South Korea, too, if it's possible."

"Is that right? I do know a missionary who helps North Korean refugees go to the South."

Nam-sik moved closer to the old man and sat down right beside him.

"A missionary, you said?" he asked. "What does a missionary do?"

"Oh, a missionary is someone who believes in God," Mr. Choi said. "The missionary I'm talking about is Mr. Park. His work is helping North Korean refugees."

"You're being serious, aren't you, Mr. Choi? If I ask Mr. Park for help, will he take me to South Korea? I want to go to South Korea. Mr. Choi, can you ask the missionary to take me to South Korea?"

Mr. Choi seemed to be mulling something over in his head. After a while, he nodded.

"All right," he said. "I'd better call him to find out where he is."

Mr. Choi picked up the phone and dialed a number. Before long, someone answered on the other end. Yeong-dae and Nam-sik leaned forward and tried to hear what was being said. After a short conversation, Mr. Choi hung up.

"Well, it just so happens that Mr. Park will be passing through this village in a few days," the man said. "Do you boys really want to go to South Korea?"

"I can't go, Mr. Choi!" Yeong-dae blurted out in answer to the question. "I have to find my sister first. Mr. Choi, can you please help me find my sister?"

As Yeong-dae begged the old man to help him, tears came to his eyes.

Mr. Choi thought Yeong-dae's request over carefully and then answered.

"We don't have a lot of time," he told Yeong-dae. "Mr. Park always moves according to plan. If you two decide you want to go to South Korea, you might have to leave right away. At any rate, we can work out the details when I get back from

Wangqing."

The next day, as Mr. Choi got ready to head to Wangqing, he had Yeong-dae describe how old his sister was and what she looked like.

Yeong-dae was excited at the thought that he might find his older sister soon.

"Nam-sik, when we find my sister, we can go to South Korea and eat as much rice as we want," he promised.

"You bet! I'm definitely going to South Korea," Nam-sik said. "Since I was young, I'd heard about South Korea from my father. But now that I've seen it on TV here, I know for sure."

"You'll run into a lot of risks on your way to South Korea," Mrs. Choi told Nam-sik with caution in her voice. "The Chinese police are a threat, of course. Also, you never know how long it'll take. There are a lot of North Koreans who spend years in China waiting for their chance to go to South Korea. It's a long and dangerous journey, so you have to be very careful. You aren't safe without a reliable guide. Fortunately, we know Mr. Park. You can count on him."

Yeong-dae was still too preoccupied with his sister to give much thought to anything else.

"Wouldn't it be great if Mr. Choi found my sister?" he said, thinking aloud. "I don't even know if she's still alive. If I could just see her once, I wouldn't ask for anything else."

"I've just got to go to South Korea with you and Yeong-ran," he said, turning to his friend. "Nam-sik, my heart is so full, it could burst!"

Yeong-dae's eyes were glued to the door all day as he waited for Mr. Choi to return with some good news.

The old man came back late that night. As soon as he stepped in the door, he noticed Yeong-dae staring at his face, trying to read his expression. It was clear how eager the boy was to hear the news.

"In the village where I went to visit my acupuncture patient," he began after shutting the door, "they say there are three North Korean women married to Chinese men. All three of them were abducted and sold to the men. One of those women was brought here three years ago, and they say she has a baby boy. She's the youngest of the three, and she's supposed to be from Kilju. I guess she's around your sister's age, but I didn't have a chance to see her. Her husband's bad-tempered, and he never lets her go outside."

When Yeong-dae heard this, tears came to his eyes.

"So you mean she's locked up like some kind of criminal?"

"He's not the only Chinese man who treats his North Korean wife like that," Mr. Choi explained. "They all watch their wives carefully to make sure they don't run away. Since the women were kidnapped, I guess it makes sense that they would want to run away, right? But it seems like this guy is pretty extreme even for someone who bought a North Korean woman."

Yeong-dae felt sure that his sister Yeong-ran must be locked up by the man Mr. Choi was describing. If she did come from Kilju three years ago, who else could it be?

"Can you let me know how to get there, Mr. Choi?" Yeong-dae asked. "If you describe in detail which house they live in, I'll go there right away and find out whether the woman is my sister or not."

Yeong-dae's heart ached with concern for his poor sister.

"Mr. Choi," Nam-sik interrupted, "did you ask the missionary to take us with him?"

"If everything goes according to plan, he said he'd visit here in the evening two days from now," the man responded. "Mr. Park always has to watch out for the Chinese police, so he could get here a day or two late. But whatever the case, we don't have a lot of time."

When he heard this, Nam-sik swallowed nervously.

"Yeong-dae, you better hurry back," the older boy said. "When the missionary Mr. Choi told us about gets here, I'm going with him no matter what."

Yeong-dae was taken aback by this.

"Nam-sik, you're not going to make me look for my sister by myself, are you?"

Just then, the phone rang. Mr. Choi picked it up at once. Sure enough, it was Mr. Park.

"Mr. Park said that he's coming to pick the two of you up in the evening the day after tomorrow," the old man said. "He told us to get ready."

"The day after tomorrow?" Yeong-dae repeated anxiously. "Mr. Choi, can't he come any later than that?"

"No, he can't," the old man said. "You boys aren't the only ones he's taking with him. Anyway, Mr. Park doesn't work by himself. There are people here and there who help him out. He has to work around their schedules, so he can't just drop everything because you want him to. You should just be grateful that he's taking you with him at all."

Yeong-dae wished that he could've left for Wangqing that very moment.

The Trip to Wangqing

Yeong-dae kept pleading with Nam-sik until late that night.

"Nam-sik, you don't expect me to go by myself, do you? I'm scared! Please, Nam-sik, just come with me until I get to Wangqing. You can hide and keep a lookout while I go by myself to the house where my sister's supposed to be. OK, Nam-sik? You can do this for me, can't you?"

Nam-sik was hesitant, but at last, he nodded his head.

"OK, Yeong-dae," he said. "I have to admit, I felt a little guilty about the idea of you heading off by yourself. I want to go with you to South Korea. We'll make our way to Wangqing early tomorrow morning."

When Nam-sik said this, Yeong-dae was finally able to relax.

The next morning, Mr. Choi gave Yeong-dae all of the information he needed to get to Wangqing and how to find the house where the North Korean woman was said to be living. He also gave the two boys bus fare for their journey and urged them again and again to be extra careful.

"I hope this doesn't happen," the old man said, "but if you do get detained by the police, you mustn't say that you were at our house. If you're caught, you and I have to act like we don't know each other, even if we happen to see each other again. Do you understand what I'm saying?"

Yeong-dae said he did understand. In China, hiding North Korean refugees was against the law.

Explaining that the two boys' accents marked them as North Koreans, Mr. Choi urged them not to talk at all in front of other people.

Yeong-dae packed all of his belongings in his backpack just in case he might need something on the journey. He wrapped the notebook that Yeong-ran had given him inside some old clothes. The old woman put a hat on Yeong-dae's head. He needed to look Chinese, she said.

Yeong-dae felt nervous when he got on the bus with Nam-sik and throughout the ride to Wangqing. He tried his best to avoid making eye contact with anyone else. In North Korea, buses were very irregular because of fuel shortages. But this Chinese bus rolled into Wangqing just when it was scheduled to arrive.

Yeong-dae and Nam-sik explored the town with the map that Mr. Choi had drawn for them, trying to find the neighborhood where the North Korean woman was said to be living. Since most of the houses looked very similar to each other, they had to pull the map out every few minutes to check their location. When they were on a road with a lot of people on it, they walked fast, pretending to be in a great hurry.

After about an hour of wandering around, the two boys located the neighborhood that the old man had told them about. They counted the houses one by one, glancing down at the map and then slowly looking around them. At last, they saw the house where the North Korean woman was supposed to be living. Yeong-dae was on pins and needles. He wanted to believe that his sister was really there.

Yeong-dae and Nam-sik hid in a cluster of trees a short distance from the house and waited for it to get dark. There seemed to be nobody going in or out of the house. Maybe the Chinese man didn't even let his child go outside.

More than three years had passed since Yeong-dae's sister had run away from home, and his mind was full of questions. How had she changed during that time? Was she really in the house? Was it true that she couldn't leave and was always being watched like some kind of criminal? They said she'd had a son. Did that make her a mother? When she met Yeong-dae, would she want to run away with him? What would they do with her son?

Yeong-dae didn't have any good ideas about what to do even if he did eventually find his sister. If the woman here was really Yeong-ran, what would he tell Chang-u when he saw him? Yeong-dae's head was spinning. But at any rate, the first thing he had to worry about was finding his sister.

"Nam-sik, stay here," Yeong-dae said, grabbing Nam-sik's hand and squeezing it. "I'm going to go to the house and find out whether Yeong-ran is there or not. If by any chance something goes wrong, I want you to go on back to Mr. Choi's house. Go back and . . ."

Yeong-dae choked up and couldn't finish. It sounded too much like he was saying goodbye to Nam-sik.

Nam-sik nodded his head.

"You better not get caught, Yeong-dae!" he said. "I'll hide

here and wait until you get back. Go on! Be careful."

Nam-sik hugged Yeong-dae fiercely and then slapped him on the back. After taking a deep breath, Yeong-dae started walking toward the house. He was on edge and kept glancing behind him where Nam-sik was hiding. Nam-sik mouthed the words "be careful" one last time.

Yeong-dae waved at his friend in return and then cautiously moved forward. When he made it to the fence in front of the house, a dog inside the fence began barking savagely. Surprised by the sound, Yeong-dae stopped dead in his tracks. He hadn't thought that there'd be a dog there. The more he moved, the louder the dog barked, but he couldn't just stand there, either.

Yeong-dae quickly slipped away from the sound, along the fence to where it connected with the wall of the house. The dog barked even louder, but didn't come out of the gate after him. The dog must be tied up, Yeong-dae guessed. This was his lucky day. When he reached the wall, he crouched and waited. A faint light could be seen through a window near him. Yeong-dae listened carefully for any sounds that might be coming from inside the house. The dog was still barking. From time to time, a shadow would pass across the window and then vanish. Yeong-dae made up his mind to stay there until the dog became quiet.

After some time, the dog yelped one last time and then stopped barking. Rising from his crouch, Yeong-dae crept along the wall on his tip-toes, moving toward the lighted window. One step, two steps, three steps—and then his foot connected with an empty glass bottle, which rolled across the ground with a clatter.

Almost at once, he heard a door bang open, and someone started shouting.

"*Ni shi shei?*"[12]

It was a deep voice—a man's voice—and he was speaking Chinese. Yeong-dae's heart almost stopped. His feet seemed to be made of lead. He couldn't move.

The gate in the fence opened, and he heard the man's gruff voice right behind him.

"*Bie dong!*"[13]

At the same moment, a black dog charged at Yeong-dae. Yeong-dae screamed and fell forward, right on his face. The snarling dog locked its sharp teeth into Yeong-dae's pants leg and shook it from side to side.

---

12. "Who are you?" in Chinese.

13. "Don't move!" in Chinese

Yeong-dae was blinded by a sudden glare. Someone was shining a flashlight directly into his eyes. It was so bright that Yeong-dae couldn't see anything else.

The man was shouting something in Chinese. Yeong-dae squeezed his eyes shut. The man grabbed the boy by his collar and yanked him up into the air. Yeong-dae dangled from the man's powerful grip like a helpless baby. The man pulled Yeong-dae behind him through the gate and into the yard, where he flung him down onto the hard ground. Yeong-dae fell painfully on his butt. The man tied Yeong-dae's hands behind him with nylon string. Yeong-dae was in so much pain that he could hardly breathe. The man kept shouting at Yeong-dae and shaking his finger at him. Yeong-dae didn't understand a single word of Chinese. He'd been caught like a rat in a trap!

With an effort, Yeong-dae raised his head and looked over toward the house, with the light shining through the windows.

Yeong-ran, please come out! I'm here!

Yeong-dae made a silent, desperate appeal to his sister.

The man opened Yeong-dae's backpack and flipped it upside down, sending all the old clothes and other possessions in the bag tumbling to the ground. He shined his flashlight on the items one by one, looking them over closely.

That was when Yeong-dae had an awful realization. The map that Mr. Choi had drawn for him and the notebook he'd gotten from his sister were both in the bag. If the man saw the map, his suspicions would be confirmed. Sure enough, when the man picked up the map, he scowled and glanced over at Yeong-dae with a menacing look.

The man raised his voice again, but this time he seemed to be talking to someone else. Of course, it was all in Chinese, so Yeong-dae couldn't understand any of it. Just then, Yeong-dae heard a child crying from inside the house. His heart started racing. He desperately hoped that his sister would come out of the door. But no one came to the door.

Yeong-ran! Hurry and come out. Hurry!

Maybe Yeong-ran was so startled by Yeong-dae's arrival that she didn't know what to do. Yeong-dae hoped so badly that she'd open the door, come outside, and recognize him.

At last, the door opened, and a woman stepped into the yard. Eyes wide and heart pounding like a drum, Yeong-dae stared at the silhouette of the woman in front of the light pouring out of the doorway. The woman spoke to the man in hesitant Chinese. But it wasn't his sister's voice. Yeong-ran had a long, graceful neck; this woman's neck was so squat that she barely seemed to have a neck at all.

All of Yeong-dae's hopes were shattered. Just then, he remembered Nam-sik.

What's Nam-sik doing? He must know that I've been caught. What should I do?

The man tore up the map that Mr. Choi had drawn and flung the pieces on the ground. Then he flipped through the notebook that Yeong-dae's sister had given him. Would the man be able to tell that it was written in Korean? Yeong-dae's pulse was racing.

After a moment, the man went inside the house and picked up the phone to make a call. After the call was over, he came outside again and put Yeong-dae in a little shed in the yard. From the light of the flashlight, the boy could see farm tools lying around inside the shed. Then the door shut, and he heard a rattle. Yeong-dae guessed the man had locked it.

Tears rolled down Yeong-dae's cheeks. The woman here wasn't his sister.

One way or another, I have to find Nam-sik and get back to Mr. Choi's house. . . What am I going to do?

Yeong-dae struggled with the nylon cord around his wrists, trying to free his hands. But the more he struggled, the more his wrists hurt. And even if he did get his hands free, the door was still locked so he couldn't get away.

Sometime later, the dog started barking again outside. Yeong-dae wondered if Nam-sik had come to find him. He fumbled around in the black space, trying to find the door. The dog was still barking angrily. Yeong-dae called out to Nam-sik in a low voice.

"Nam-sik! Is that you?"

There was no response. That awful dog was barking even louder. Just then, Yeong-dae heard the front door of the house slam open.

"Ni shi shei?" the man shouted in Chinese.

Yeong-dae was afraid that Nam-sik would be caught, too. Through a crack in the door, he saw the flicker of the flashlight beam. He could hear the pounding of footsteps. The man shouted again outside.

"Ni gan shenme?"[14]

Nam-sik must've run off after sneaking in to look at the shed. Yeong-dae stamped his feet on the ground in frustration. After a while, he heard footsteps again. Then the front door opened

---

14. "What are you doing?" in Chinese

and shut, and it grew quiet again. Even the dog had stopped barking. Leaning against the door post, Yeong-dae kept trying to free his hands from the cord, but it was tied too tight. Soon, his skin felt like it was burning from the constant chafing. In the end, he slumped to the floor and fell asleep.

The next thing he knew, a car engine was humming outside. Yeong-dae guessed that it was the next morning. When the engine stopped, the dog began making noise again. Yeong-dae heard the sound of a door opening and people's footsteps coming closer. Several people were chattering in Chinese.

The door of the shed opened, and the man from last night reached in and dragged Yeong-dae outside. Once his eyes adjusted to the light, he saw two uniformed men, both in hats, and one with glasses on. Since they were wearing the same uniforms and hats, it seemed clear that they were police officers.

Yeong-dae felt like he was about to faint. The man in glasses looked at Yeong-dae and asked him something in Chinese. When Yeong-dae didn't answer, the officer turned to the owner of the house and repeated the question. Pointing at Yeong-dae, the owner spoke at some length in Chinese. Yeong-dae couldn't understand a thing.

Yeong-dae looked around, worried about what had happened to Nam-sik. Where had he hidden? Had he gone back to Mr. Choi's house by himself? He peered around in every direction, but Nam-sik was nowhere to be seen.

After he finished what he was saying to the man in glasses, the owner of the house gestured to Yeong-dae with his chin. The man with glasses searched the boy's body. He seemed to be looking for some kind of identification. When he couldn't find anything, he looked at Yeong-dae's notebook. Yeong-dae felt sure that the man would figure out he was from North Korea just by looking at the notebook.

Sure enough, the next thing the man in glasses did was put handcuffs on Yeong-dae's hands. Now Yeong-dae was really in a bind.

The man in glasses took Yeong-dae out of the yard to where the car had been parked next to the house. After forcing him to sit in the backseat of the car, the man handed some money to the owner of the house. Yeong-dae had no way of knowing how much it was, but he could tell that it was Chinese currency. It looked like the owner had earned some money for reporting Yeong-dae to the police.

I'm done for, Yeong-dae thought. He'd heard that the Chinese police could spot a North Korean just by looking at them. And then there was the notebook. He was in a real jam now.

Yeong-dae looked out through the windows of the car. The police started the engine. Yeong-dae felt extremely anxious. He kept looking toward the woods where Nam-sik had been hiding. The car pulled away from the house. Yeong-dae could not tear his eyes away from the window.

Nam-sik, what are we going to do? I got caught. Help me, Nam-sik!

Just then, he saw Nam-sik crouched down behind a big pine tree. Yeong-dae's heart pounded, but the car kept moving. He couldn't say goodbye to Nam-sik like this! All of a sudden, Yeong-dae squirmed out of his seat and tried to stick his head out of the open window. But as soon as he moved, the policeman in the seat next to him struck him with his baton. Yeong-dae tried to dodge the blow, but he was hit in the face and fell back into his seat.

Yeong-dae felt warm liquid spreading across his face. His nose was bleeding. His chest heaved as he cried quietly, and he looked back at the pine grove where Nam-sik was standing. Nam-sik had come out onto the road and was looking at Yeong-dae with tears rolling down his cheeks.

Nam-sik, hurry and go back to Mr. Choi. I want you to go to South Korea, even if you have to go by yourself. Good-bye, Nam-sik!

Yeong-dae was afraid to look at Nam-sik anymore. He thought the police might notice his friend. His nose was still bleeding, but he couldn't wipe the blood away because his hands were cuffed. His cheeks were smeared with a mess of tears and blood. He furtively looked out the window but couldn't see Nam-sik anymore. He continued to cry.

Eventually, the police car stopped in front of a building. Out front was a flagpole with the red Chinese flag fluttering at the top. The building looked like a Chinese police station. The police car had parked next to several motorcycles with little Chinese flags attached to them as well. The police opened the car door and roughly hauled Yeong-dae out the way they might have moved a bag of groceries. The boy stumbled and nearly smacked his face on the pavement.

The police escorted Yeong-dae into the building. Several men were doing work at their desks. Two men sitting in tall chairs rose to their feet as soon as they saw Yeong-dae.

"Well, look what we have here!" one of them said.

Yeong-dae was taken aback. The two were speaking Korean.

He looked closer and saw little badges bearing Kim Jong-il's face pinned to their uniforms. They were North Korean police officers.

The Detention Center Outside of North Korea

When Yeong-dae saw the North Korean police, his blood ran cold.

He'd been taken to a Chinese jail. Around the jail was a high wall, and next to the gate were standing soldiers carrying guns. Inside the jail was a long corridor with metal doors on both sides. Yeong-dae could see prisoners through the bars. In each of the cells was a security camera and two heavy doors.

On the walls of the cells, North Korean defectors had scribbled messages.

If we're going to survive, we've got to reform and liberalize the country!

I miss my mom.

Don't believe what the Chinese tell you.

I'll never stop leaving North Korea and searching for freedom.

Years of scribbling had nearly turned the gray walls black.

There were many more North Korean women than men in the jail. Yeong-dae craned his neck and peered toward the area where the women were held. He wondered if they'd have any news about Yeong-ran.

A guard wrote Yeong-dae's name on a piece of paper.

"When did you cross the river?" he asked in a brusque voice.

When Yeong-dae hesitated, the guard's voice grew even meaner.

"Answer the question, boy," he growled. "When did you cross the river?"

Yeong-dae told him he'd come across three days ago.

"Why did you go to Wangqing?" the guard asked. "Who were you trying to see at that house?"

"I was hungry, so I wanted to get something to eat."

As soon as Yeong-dae said this, the guard kicked him.

"How dare you go around bringing shame on our country!"

He smacked Yeong-dae across the face.

"Listen up carefully, and tell me the truth. Did you meet the South Koreans or not?"

Yeong-dae wasn't sure what to make of the sudden question. The guard started yelling again.

"If you want to get out of here alive, you'd better answer me. I want to know whether you got in touch with the South Koreans or not. Tell me now! Did you meet them, or didn't you?"

Yeong-dae shook his head vigorously.

"I don't know anything about that," Yeong-dae said. "I just wanted to find something to eat because I was hungry. I was planning on going back to our country."

"You went all the way to Wangqing to find something to eat? You expect me to believe that story? Why did you go to that house?"

Yeong-dae stuck to the same answer.

"You have to believe me. I just wanted to find some food because I was hungry. I was going to return to our country."

Yeong-dae begged the guard for mercy, but he hauled the boy to a prison cell and shoved him in. It wasn't a big cell to begin with, but more than 20 people had somehow been crammed inside. The cell door was locked with a metal chain, and there was one small window that opened onto the outside world. The people in the cell were wearing old, worn-out clothing, and they were bruised and cut as if they'd been beaten. One man was slumped over to his side, with dried blood on his foot.

"Sit up straight, damn it!" the guard told the prisoner who was on his side and kicked him.

In the cell, the prisoners had to relieve themselves—both liquid and solid—in a big pail. Whenever the lid was raised, the stench was so awful that Yeong-dae could barely breathe. Each time a guard walked by outside the cell, the people inside cried out pitifully.

"Please help us! If they send us back, we'll die. Please let us stay in China."

But the guards either ignored these appeals or hit the door with their batons and told the prisoners to shut up.

The notebook that Yeong-dae's sister had given him just made things worse for him during interrogations with the guards.

"This notebook is from South Korea," one guard said. "You little brat, you met the South Korean agents, didn't you?"

Every time the guards questioned him, Yeong-dae answered the same way. He'd crossed the river because he was hungry, he told them. He lost count of how many times he wished he hadn't brought that notebook

Whenever more North Korean defectors were brought to the prison, Yeong-dae worried about Nam-sik. Could Nam-sik have made it to South Korea by himself? When no one was looking, Yeong-dae wrote a note on the wall in a corner of the cell.

Nam-sik, I'm here! — Yeong-dae

But the wall was covered with so many black scribbles that the message could hardly be read.

Three months later, Yeong-dae was taken to a detention center in Tumen, a city on the border with North Korea. The guards chained the refugees together in one long line and made them climb up on the bed of a truck. Yeong-dae sat down at the very back of the truck.

As soon as they were all aboard, the guard transporting them shouted a command.

"Heads down! All of you!"

When they heard this, all the prisoners on the truck kneeled down on the truck bed and lowered their heads.

The truck started moving. Curious about where they were going, Yeong-dae lifted his head to take a peek.

Suddenly, a whip cracked across his back.

"You little traitor," the guard said. "You have some nerve

lifting your head like that!"

Yeong-dae's back stung where the whip had hit him. He covered his face with his cuffed hands. He felt like a cow being led to the slaughterhouse.

After a while, the guard stopped yelling, and Yeong-dae worked up the courage to look out of the truck again. They were passing through a mid-size city. Large buildings lined both of the roads. A lot of billboards had Korean words written below Chinese characters. They passed a signpost that said "Nampingjin, Helong, Jilin Province."

The truck left the city and lumbered for some time down a path lined by tall pine trees. Seeing the pine trees made Yeong-dae think of the night a few months back when he and Nam-sik had crossed the river and walked through the woods.

After some time on the road, Yeong-dae saw the North Korean city of Namyang in North Hamgyong Province across the river and off in the distance. Then they came to the Tumen Bridge, which linked China with North Korea. Peach blossoms were in full bloom on one side of the road. It was spring, and they were passing by an orchard. But it didn't feel like spring to Yeong-dae. Ever since the Chinese police had caught him, his heart had been trapped in a mid-winter blizzard.

The truck stopped within sight of the Tumen Bridge. As soon as the prisoners got out of the truck, the guards told all of them to walk in line with their heads down and their eyes on the heels of the person in front of them. When one of the prisoners lifted his head, a guard struck him with his whip, causing the prisoner to flinch and then stumble. At this, the guard pulled out his truncheon and gave him a blow to the back, knocking him over. Since all of the prisoners were tied to the same rope, the people in front and behind fell down, too.

As soon as the prisoners reached the detention center, they were all given numbers. Yeong-dae was No. 7. The cells were really only big enough for five or six people to lie down side by side, but the guards put thirty people in each room. People were jammed into the tiny room as tightly as sardines in a can. Yeong-dae's head ached from the smell of bad breath, sweat, and piss. There was no window, and he felt like he was suffocating.

The guards told them to hand over all their safety pins, leather belts, and even the elastic bands on their boxers and pants. Yeong-dae could hear some older men whispering to each other right behind him.

"They're afraid we might kill ourselves," one said. "They take away anything that could be used to commit suicide."

"Dying would be better than being dragged back to our country."

"You're right. Suicide would be a no-brainer for anyone who's had to go through this before."

The two men's whispers scared Yeong-dae even more.

The only food the prisoners were given was a few ground kernels of corn and a couple of beans. But on their first day in the cell, they had to even give that up to the head prisoner in the room. If they didn't, the head prisoner said, he'd beat them up. This frightened Yeong-dae, so he handed over all his food just like the head prisoner said.

The guards spent several days searching the bodies of the prisoners thoroughly, pocketing any money or valuables that they found. Yeong-dae heard that the women had an even harder time of it. Apparently women had more places in their bodies to hide money than men did. Yeong-dae got frequent cramps in his legs from spending the entire night in a sitting position. There wasn't enough space to stretch his legs out, so the best he could do was massage his legs. One night while he was doing this, a man with a shaggy beard started thrashing around and screaming.

"This is No. 24! My stomach is killing me!"

The guard opened the door and yelled for him to come out.

Hardly breathing and with his face pale, No. 24 managed to crawl out of the cell.

"That guy swallowed his money," someone near Yeong-dae was whispering. "He rolled up some money, stuffed it in a plastic bag and swallowed it. Looks like it got stuck somewhere inside him."

"That's too bad," someone responded. "I guess the wad of money was too big. Poor guy. That money may be the death of him."

"He's not the only one who swallowed money, I bet!"

Angry muttering could be heard all around the cell. The guards had been busy over the past few days examining the bodies of the prisoners and trying to locate hidden valuables.

The prisoners at the detention center were forced to sit in the same place from five in the morning to ten at night. They were allowed to get up for two minutes every two hours. Each time they stretched their arms and legs, all of their joints cracked.

A few days later, one of the guards ordered Yeong-dae to come out of the cell.

He'd been sitting for so long that when he got up, he nearly fell back down again.

"Be quick about it, dammit!" the guard shouted when he saw Yeong-dae trying to stand up. "Stop your dawdling!"

Frightened, Yeong-dae hurried over to the guard. The guard handed him a long stick with a hook at the end of it. Yeong-dae wasn't sure what he was supposed to do with this until the guard led him over to where all the buckets of excrement from the cells were lined up.

"Starting today, you're going to stir these buckets with the stick and look for wads of money," the guard said. "Listen up, boy. Any funny business, and you're going to be drinking that slop! You should be grateful that I'm giving you an easy job."

Yeong-dae couldn't believe what he was hearing. Most defectors who were caught swallowed money so that they could bribe their way to freedom when taken back to North Korea. The guards were so good at finding money that the prisoners hid on their person that they had no choice but to stick the money in a plastic bag and swallow it. The prisoners would wait until the bags came out the other end while relieving themselves and then hide them again. Sometimes, though, they failed to grab the money bags before they fell into the bucket. These were the bags that the guard wanted Yeong-dae to try to find.

The putrid smell of the excrement made Yeong-dae's face pucker up. The guard started yelling at him.

"You're a capitalist, and you betrayed your country. I have every reason to make you do something that's even worse than this. So get to work and don't even *think* of trying anything funny."

It was no use disobeying the guards. Yeong-dae stirred the foul-smelling buckets with the stick and tried to find money-filled plastic bags. The guard watched Yeong-dae as he worked. When any money turned up, the guard washed the bag off and pocketed the money. The awful smell soaked into Yeong-dae's body, and he was barely able to eat anything. When he returned to the cell, he smelled so bad that prisoners beside him held their noses.

All of the prisoners at the detention center had to write confessions. They were told to say what town they were from, who their families were, where they'd gone after crossing the river, whom they met, what they did, and how they were caught. They had to write all of this in detail.

Yeong-dae didn't write about visiting the house of the old Joseonjok man or that he'd been trying to find his sister when he went to Wangqing. He said nothing about Nam-sik, either. He just wrote that he crossed the river because he was hungry, and that he ended up in Wangqing by accident in an attempt to stay away from the police.

The day after he wrote his confession, Yeong-dae was brought out of his cell again.

"Listen here, boy," the guard said. "Why didn't you write a single word here about this notebook? I guess you met some South Korean agents, eh?"

"No, sir, I didn't! I really didn't meet anyone."

"Keep your trap shut, kid! Where'd you get this notebook? Who'd you get it from?"

For several days in a row, Yeong-dae had to write the same confession over and over again. Soon, he grew sick and tired of repeatedly describing how his sister had given him the notebook.

When he handed the confession to the guard for the fifth straight day, the guard brought out all the confessions he'd written and began to compare them.

"Well, look at this, No. 7," the guard said. "Why are your confessions different?"

All of Yeong-dae's muscles went rigid. He didn't remember

what he'd written differently. The guard pulled out the first and last confessions and slapped them down in front of him.

"Take a look at this part here," the guard said, pointing to one passage in the two confessions. "These words aren't in the same order! You little brat! You're lying when you say you crossed the river because you were hungry, aren't you? Just be honest and say you met the South Korean agents!"

Without even waiting for an answer, the guard cracked his truncheon down on the boy's back. How in the world was Yeong-dae supposed to remember the exact order of the words he'd written? It was all so unfair. The guards seemed like they were questioning him just so that they'd have an excuse to beat him.

For Yeong-dae, life at the detention center was a waking nightmare. Even so, he wasn't going to let himself die there. He made up his mind to survive, whatever it took, and find his sister. By thinking about his sister, Yeong-dae was able to control his rage.

It seemed that Yeong-dae wasn't the only prisoner whose confessions didn't match. One man came back to the cell more dead than alive, while another one didn't return all day long. All of the people at the detention center were closely watching for a chance to escape, for a chance not to be taken back to North Korea.

People caught after crossing the river several times were generally sent to a prison camp or concentration camp, while people like Yeong-dae who had been caught just once ended up in labor camps or reeducation centers. For the most part, children were sent to separate detention centers for a while and then allowed to return home. But people who had tried to go to South Korea or gotten in touch with churches that help North Korean defectors were sent to political prisoner camps for life or were executed.

Inside the cell, the prisoners squabbled over the thin, filthy blankets they were given to cover themselves, and even those were crawling with lice. Anyone making noise trying to kill the lice was liable to be dragged out of the cell for a beating. When Yeong-dae saw the lice, his skin crawled. They reminded him of his younger sister Yeong-ok.

Late one night, Yeong-dae was sleeping fitfully when a cool wind seemed to touch his skin. He looked up and saw a shadow moving across the ceiling. Yeong-dae was gripped with fear. Just then, a whistle blew shrilly. The inmates in the cell who'd been asleep started to murmur together. In another moment, all the lights came on. Someone had knocked a hole in the ceiling.

Soon enough, the would-be escapee was caught. Yeong-dae heard someone say it was a young man who had tried to get to South Korea. The following day, they could hear him screaming from morning until night. He was returned to the cell after midnight, barely conscious. He muttered something about being tortured with an electric baton. Yeong-dae stared at the man, unable to move or look away.

The Detention Center Inside of North Korea

Three months later, the day came when the prisoners were brought out of the detention center on the border and taken to North Korea. As they shuffled across the Tumen Bridge, they were all shackled in one long line, just like the day when they were first brought to the center.

A crowd of people gathered alongside the road and cursed them as they passed.

"Look at those scumbags who betrayed our country! Lock 'em up and throw away the key!"

"Drown them all in the river!"

"Even a single kernel of corn is too good for the likes of these traitors!"

With his head bowed, Yeong-dae listened to the insults. All of the onlookers were chanting the same phrases together. Obviously, someone had put them up to it.

Yeong-dae and the other prisoners were taken to a jail in Namyang, Onsong County. There were ten cells for prisoners at the jail. The cells were arranged in a circle, with all of them facing a small yard in the middle. Five of the cells were used for holding captured defectors.

Once the prisoners were back in North Korea, Yeong-dae assumed they'd be treated better than in China. But he was completely wrong. At the Namyang jail, the guards treated them much more cruelly than the guards at the detention center on the border. The guards screamed at them, calling them traitors who had turned their backs on their own country.

The food was as bad as the treatment. Some days, there were more rocks in their bowls than food. When some prisoners complained about the rocks, the guards gagged them, saying even rocks were too good for people who'd betrayed their country. Every sentence that the guards spoke ended with a curse word. Anyone who dared lift his head was beaten mercilessly.

All of the guards had to be called "sir," no matter how old the prisoner or how young the guard. Each time a guard passed by, the prisoners had to bow their heads in respect. Anyone who failed to do this or made eye contact with the guards was dragged out of the cell to be punished. When the guards were too lazy to drag the prisoners out, they had them stick their hands through the bars and beat them black and blue.

Yeong-dae suffered even worse torture here than before because of the notebook his sister had bought him.

"Boy, where did this notebook come from?" the guard asked. "This wasn't made in the Republic."

"I don't know either, sir. My sister gave it to me before she was sold in China."

This made the guard fly into a rage, and he began to yell at Yeong-dae.

"What did you say? She was *sold*? The whore! You mean she wanted to have a baby with a Chinese man, don't you?"

Yeong-dae hated the guard who was insulting his sister. He hated him so much that he wanted to kill him. He really believed he'd starve or be beaten to death before they could send him to the camp for children.

Every day, Yeong-dae had to study various texts until

he could recite them from memory. He was also forced to memorize passages from his country's National Security Law. The law stipulated that those who'd been across the river illegally must never tell their countrymen what they'd seen, heard, and felt outside of North Korea. If they did, they'd be sent to prison.

Another set of texts that Yeong-dae had to memorize was the teachings of Kim Il-sung, North Korea's founder. These generally started out with the sentence, "Our comrade, the Great Leader Kim Il-sung, instructed us as follows."

When the guards finished questioning the prisoners, they put them to work. All day long, they had to move rocks, cart around sand, and pick grass. When there wasn't anything useful for them to do, they'd even be told to move rocks that they'd already moved back to their original position. When the guards gave the prisoners busy work of this sort, they always told them the same thing.

"We can't give you a spare moment, now can we? We have to keep your bodies busy all the time so that wicked thoughts have no chance to grow in your heads."

Each day felt like another day in hell. About three months after the defectors arrived, the authorities chose which of them would be sent to the concentration camp for political prisoners. All of them were adults. Some of them had worked as loggers in Russia, and others had been arrested after being overheard talking about defecting.

One of the members in this group was an old man. In a desperate attempt to avoid being sent to the concentration camp, he swallowed toxic materials, which made him violently ill. Another was a young man, only five years older than Yeong-dae, who was being sent to a political prison camp for anti-government activity. He'd been tortured so badly that he could no longer walk. The guards had to load his body on a stretcher like a corpse and carry him out.

The day after the young man was taken away, Yeong-dae was summoned from his cell. He was brought to an interrogation room and beaten within an inch of his life. It was all because of that notebook. Yeong-dae thought it was a miracle that he was still alive. The government had always insisted that South Korea was a poor country full of beggars. His notebook was proof that the government had told a pack of lies. The guards seemed inhuman to Yeong-dae. Did they truly believe the government's propaganda? Or maybe they knew that they were being fed lies but kept mistreating prisoners for fear of what might happen to them if they didn't. Yeong-dae felt anger boiling up inside of him.

Noticing the look in Yeong-dae's eyes, the guard began giving him another savage beating.

"Look at you. Your eyes are full of venom. You ought to be down on your knees begging for forgiveness. Who gave you the right to get angry? Do you want another taste of my truncheon?"

Yeong-dae could feel indignation welling up inside, but he had to keep a lid on his emotions if he wanted to be released so that he could find his sister. If he showed the slightest sign of resistance, who knew what kind of punishment he might receive? The only way to get out of this living hell was to be patient and wait.

Three months after Yeong-dae arrived at the Namyang jail, he was told that they were sending him to another jail near his old home at Kilju, North Hamgyong Province. Typically, children were released from the jail after two months, but the guards kept interrogating Yeong-dae. They continued trying to find some link to South Korea because of the notebook that his sister had given him.

Two weeks after he got the news, Yeong-dae was transferred

to the Kilju jail. Since it was the middle of winter, the streams and hills were buried under a layer of snow. He wondered sadly where his mother had been buried. He wondered what they'd done with the body of his little sister Yeong-ok. Whenever he thought of his family, he wanted to cry, but he bit his lip and resisted.

The day after Yeong-dae arrived at the jail in Kilju, the interrogations started up again. It was always the same routine, and just hearing the word "interrogation" made him want to pull his hair out. Each time, the guards had the same question for him.

"You wanted to go to South Korea, didn't you? You were working for the South Koreans from the time you got that notebook, weren't you? Tell the truth! Your sister's in South Korea, isn't she?"

"That's not true, sir," Yeong-dae said. "I didn't have any particular plan when I crossed the river. I'd just heard that I could find something to eat there. I was going to eat something and come right back to the Republic. My sister was sold to the Chinese."

Yeong-dae always said exactly the same thing, though it nearly drove him crazy.

"We don't need your lies, brat. We've had enough of your stories. Tell us where you met the South Korean agents!"

No matter how often Yeong-dae said he hadn't met any South Koreans, the guards didn't believe him. Sometimes, the torture was so hard to endure that he wanted to just lie and say he had met South Korean agents.

Sometimes the guards beat Yeong-dae with their truncheons when they got bored. Each time he was struck, he wanted to die. Certain punishments were worse than dying, Yeong-dae thought. For example, there was the "knee breaker" torture. The guards forced Yeong-dae to kneel down with a narrow wooden plank wedged behind his knees and sit there for hours at a time.

The guards took perverse pleasure in tormenting Yeong-dae. They sometimes played a game they called "pigeon." This involved pulling his hands and feet behind his back, tying them together, and then hanging him from the ceiling. Whenever they tortured him this way, Yeong-dae blacked out. Next, the guards shifted to the "fish" torture. After taking him down from the ceiling, they plunged his head into a big pot of water and held it underwater, shaking him. Yeong-dae wasn't even allowed to stay unconscious.

After the guards brought him back to the cell and left him there, he'd hear the other prisoners in the cell whispering together, talking about his plight.

"One way or another, that boy has to get out of this nightmare, and quickly!" said one of them.

"I feel so sorry for him," another responded. "They say little kids are sent to a separate prison camp. I don't understand why they keep Yeong-dae here and torture him every day. He's so pitiful that I can't bear to look at him."

"Isn't he, though? It's bad enough just watching what they do to him. Imagine what it must be like for him. Those guards can't be human. What a bunch of nasty creeps!"

"By the way, I asked my brother to bring some money for me. I have no idea why I haven't heard anything from him yet. He must've gotten my message."

This prisoner was waiting for his family to bribe the guards so that he could go free. Yeong-dae was very jealous of him.

Every day, Yeong-dae thought of his friend Nam-sik. He hoped that Nam-sik had made it to South Korea and was enjoying a good life there, but at the same time, part of him wished that his friend would come rescue him. Yeong-dae knew, of course, that this was a ridiculous fantasy but couldn't banish the thought altogether. Some nights, he dreamed about eating a tasty bowl of rice with Nam-sik. The next day, he seemed to see Nam-sik out of the corner of his eye all day long.

In early February, two months after Yeong-dae had been sent to the jail in Kilju, a guard called his name and unlocked the cell door. When the boy emerged from the cell, the guard removed his handcuffs and instructed him to take off his prison clothes. Yeong-dae was taken aback, but did as he was told.

"We're letting you go because you don't have your identification papers," the guard said as he handed him an old army uniform. "From now on, you have to be loyal to your country. Do you understand?"

Yeong-dae thought he must be dreaming.

"Sir," he said, and after a pause continued. "Does this mean that you're letting me live?"

"You're free to go. Never forget, not even for a minute, that you have to be loyal to the Party if you want to live in the embrace of the Dear Leader."

Everything had happened so suddenly that Yeong-dae's body went limp, and he collapsed in a heap on the ground.

Surely it didn't take them this long to figure out that I don't have any papers. They treated me so badly. What could this possibly mean?

After being behind bars for so long, Yeong-dae's body was slow to respond to his brain's commands. Somehow, he made it to his feet and left the jail. Once outside, a strangely familiar person approached him. Yeong-dae was stunned. It was Chang-u, the son of the local Party secretary.

"Surprised you, didn't I?" the older boy asked. "I heard from my father that you were in the Kilju jail. Did you tell them what your mother did or not?"

"No, I didn't. I didn't say anything about that. But how . . .?"

"That's a relief. If they find out about your mother, my father will be in danger, too. Don't tell anyone what happened today. You have to keep this a secret. Don't let on that you know who I am, and don't tell anyone that you saw me here. Got it?"

Seeing Chang-u made Yeong-dae think about his sister even more.

"When I saw the tragedy that your family suffered, I did a lot of thinking. I guess that Yeong-ran and I weren't meant to be together after all. I got you out of jail for your sister's sake. We'll never see each other again."

Chang-u's voice trailed off at the end. Then he pressed

something into Yeong-dae's hand and abruptly left. As Yeong-dae watched Chang-u quickly walking away, he could barely hold back the tears. When he opened his hand, he found some money there. Chang-u had shown up like a phantom and disappeared just as quickly.

I guess Chang-u is still having trouble getting over Yeong-ran. If she hadn't run away from home, she and Chang-u might have gotten married. Where could my sister be?

Yeong-dae stuffed the money Chang-u had given him into his pocket. He walked and then walked some more, putting some distance between himself and the jail. He kept tripping as he walked. The army uniform they had given him was so loose it felt like he was wearing a big sack.

It was February, but the weather was still cold, and Yeong-dae couldn't stop shivering. After spending more than a year in various jails and detention centers, he was emaciated.

Exactly three and a half years had passed since Yeong-dae had left the house. He hobbled along, looking and feeling even weaker than during his days as a *kkotjebi*. Barely conscious, he managed to make it to his old neighborhood. When he reached the desolate ruins of his old house, he fainted.

Back at the Old House

Far, far away, Yeong-dae could hear someone calling his name. The voice gradually grew louder. He seemed to feel the warmth of someone's hand. With great effort, Yeong-dae managed to open his eyes. Mrs. Kim, his neighbor, was shaking him and calling his name.

"You very nearly froze to death," she told him. "Where have you been and how did you get in such a state? Good grief, Yeong-dae, you're nothing but skin and bones. You were barely breathing, and I wasn't sure whether you were dead or alive. I carried you to my house and put you to bed. As cold as it is, if you'd gone to sleep out there, who knows what would have happened to you."

As he tried to remember everything that had happened, Yeong-dae looked around him. He was in his neighbor's house. When Mrs. Kim found Yeong-dae collapsed in front of his house, she took him to her own home and laid him down in a warm bed. She told him how she'd kept rubbing him until he stopped shivering.

Yeong-dae remembered staggering in a daze toward his house and then blacking out right in front of it. As he took a bite of the corn porridge that Mrs. Kim had cooked for him, he started to feel like himself again.

"You poor boy," the woman fretted. "All of us villagers ought to have taken care of you and your sister when you lost your parents. I feel so bad that we couldn't do that for you. Not that things have been much easier for us, either. We manage to get by, one day at a time. By the way, Yeong-dae, Yeong-ran was here."

When Yeong-dae heard his sister's name, he jumped to his feet, but he was so weak that he had to sit back down again.

"When was she here? Was my sister OK? Where's she now?" He blurted out questions, eager to learn what had happened.

"She kept her visit a secret from everyone. She was here to see her family, but she left as soon as I told her that you'd crossed the river looking for her. I don't know what happened after that."

"When did she come by? When was she here, Mrs. Kim?"

So his sister was alive after all! Just knowing that Yeong-ran was alive made him feel stronger.

"Mrs. Kim, how was Yeong-ran? She wasn't sick, was she? Where did she say she'd been? Did she tell you that she hadn't been sold in China?"

"Slow down, Yeong-dae, I can't even get a word in edgewise! Your sister was kidnapped and sold, but somehow managed to escape. After that, she hid in a city called Shenyang. I don't know all the details, but she was arrested by the Chinese police when she went back to the place where she'd been sold. She said she was sent to prison but managed to get out and come here. Your sister said she learned hairdressing while in Shenyang. She was crying so hard that she wasn't able to tell me much."

Yeong-dae felt a lump in his throat.

So you were sold after all. Poor Yeong-ran! Everything they said about feeding you rice and getting you a job was a lie.

"Mrs. Kim," Yeong-dae told his neighbor. "Did Yeong-ran say where she was going? Did she leave some kind of message for me?"

"She headed off right away, saying she was going to find you. She probably went back to Shenyang."

It took Yeong-dae a few days to regain complete use of his body. On the third day, he finally felt well enough to leave Mrs. Kim's house. First, he visited his father's grave. With no one around to take care of it, the cemetery had been overrun by weeds, and it took Yeong-dae a long time to find his father's grave. The burial mound was in terrible shape. Rain had eroded some of the dirt, and grass covered the mound. Yeong-dae picked the grass with his bare hands and then bowed before the grave.

Father, I'm sorry I couldn't take care of Mom and Yeong-ok. You have to help me find Yeong-ran. When I cross the river this time, it's going to be hard to find her. Father, I'm going to find Yeong-ran, and we're going to go to South Korea. I want to go to South Korea and live a decent life. Please keep watch over me, Father . . . Father.

As the words echoed in his head, heavy tears welled up in his eyes and dropped to the ground.

After Yeong-dae got back from the graveyard, he said goodbye to Mrs. Kim. Before leaving, he asked her to tell

Yeong-ran — if she happened to get in touch — that he'd gone to Shenyang to look for her. Yeong-dae also wanted to thank Chang-u for everything that he'd done for him. But since the older boy had told him they had to act as if they didn't know each other, Yeong-dae had no way to express his gratitude.

Before crossing the river into China again, Yeong-dae wanted to visit Chongjin to find out what had happened to Nam-sik. If Nam-sik had been arrested and released, he might have gone looking for Geun-bae, Yeong-dae figured.

I wonder if Geun-bae is still at Sunam Market. Did anything happen to Geun-bae's little sister Song-hwa? I hope that her frostbitten feet are better now.

Just the thought of seeing Geun-bae was a relief for Yeong-dae.

As he made his way to Sunam Market, Yeong-dae was full of mixed emotions. It was hard to shake the feeling that his mother and older sister were doing business somewhere in the marketplace. When he saw parents walking through the market with their children, he was reminded of when he, his parents, and his two sisters had all been together. He found himself imagining that he heard Yeong-ok's happy laughter somewhere in the distance.

When Yeong-dae got to Sunam Market, it was as crowded as ever. He headed below the bridge where he and the other *kkotjebi* had stayed. But neither Geun-bae nor Song-hwa was underneath the bridge. Yeong-dae roved through the back alleys around the market, but he didn't see a single familiar face. All of a sudden, he missed his days as a *kkotjebi*. Sure, he'd lived like a beggar, but at least he'd had Yeong-ok. Yeong-dae looked at the sky above him and whispered his sister's name.

I'm sorry, Yeong-ok. Wherever you are now, I bet you're not hungry or cold. Are you with Mom and Dad? I'm so sorry.

Yeong-dae's eyes blurred over with tears. He wanted to learn of Nam-sik's whereabouts, but there was no one here he could ask.

Yeong-dae got on board the train for Musan once again. Since he didn't have a travel pass, he got caught and kicked off the train several times, but now it was easy for him to grab hold of the train as it was departing and clamber on board again.

When the train stopped at Cholsan, just a short distance from Musan, Yeong-dae got caught by the conductor one more time. This time, the attendants kept an eye on him, and he wasn't able to sneak aboard the train before it left. Instead, Yeong-dae had to walk the last twenty leagues from Cholsan to Musan.

As a rule, Yeong-dae only moved at night. Using the money Chang-u had given him, he bought some extra food for emergencies. He couldn't believe how lucky he was.

This time, Yeong-dae had to cross the river by himself. Since the ice over the river had thawed, he'd have to swim, but the water was still too cold for that. For about a month, Yeong-dae stayed in Musan, living like a *kkotjebi* as he waited for the weather to warm up.

Finally, the catkins on the willows next to the river began to bloom. Yeong-dae could hardly wait to cross the river. He found a spot far from the border guard station and decided to make the crossing from there. He'd have to swim the river in the black of night when no one could see him. Since Yeong-dae had swum in the ocean when visiting his grandmother's house as a child, he wasn't too worried about his swimming ability.

Yeong-dae made up his mind to cross the river on a night when it was drizzling. If it rained too much, the water level could rise. This would make the crossing more dangerous, but the rain might also keep the guards from making their rounds.

One night, the rain started drizzling just as Yeong-dae had wanted. He took off his clothes and wrapped them with his other possessions in a plastic sheet. He then stuffed the bundle into a big, heavy-duty plastic bag and blew air into it. The plastic bag inflated just like a life preserver.

Wearing nothing but his underwear, Yeong-dae dipped his big toe in the river. The water was as cold as ice. He slowly began to ease into the water, moving carefully to keep water out of the plastic bag. Soon, he was in the water up to his knees. The current was stronger than he'd expected, making it hard to move forward. The further he moved toward the middle of the river, the deeper the water got. The river kept pushing him downstream. It took all of his strength to forge ahead.

When the water was lapping around his neck, a light appeared. Yeong-dae stopped where he was and ducked his head underwater. The beam of light was moving here and there above him. The boy held his breath for some time, waiting under the water. If he made a sound — if he stuck his head above the water and the flashlight beam found him — everything was over. He wouldn't let himself die, not now! He was angry enough about the difficult life he had led until then. He wished he could've found a tube or hose to breathe under water. But wishing wouldn't help him now. Somehow, he had to survive.

Yeong-dae slowly raised his head above the water to suck in some air. While he inhaled, he watched the bright flashlight beams flickering around him. He dipped his head below the surface again like a turtle. At that moment, a whistle blew shrilly. With a desperate effort, he swam forward below the water. The middle of the river was deep. Holding his breath, he kept swimming through the water toward the other side. He could still hear the whistle blowing.

Yeong-dae's lungs were aching from holding his breath for so long. After sticking his head out of the water again and gasping for air, he tried to touch the bottom with his feet, but it was still too deep. His lungs full once more, he ducked below the surface and started swimming again. Just when he was about to faint from lack of air, he felt something hard under his feet. He was touching the bottom. Yeong-dae waded forward through the water and reached the riverbank. He felt like his heart would explode. He heard the bang of a gun being fired somewhere behind him. He kept running and didn't stop.

He didn't know how far he'd run, but the gunshots seemed to have stopped. Yeong-dae flopped down in the thick grass.

Across the river, flashlight beams were waving back and forth. Faintly, he seemed to hear someone screaming. Someone else must've been caught trying to cross the river. He breathed a long sigh of relief.

Yeong-dae was back in China at last! In the distance, he saw car lights that gradually got closer. He dropped down and lay flat in the grass. He'd been told that Chinese police stopped their cars on the main roads to look for defectors. He was sure this was the police. With relief, he watched as the headlights swept past where he was crouching in the grass and then vanished.

Instead of following the main road, Yeong-dae walked down a narrow path in the woods to stay hidden. When he crossed the river with Nam-sik, it had been the middle of winter, and he'd been cold and scared. But now, there were leaves on the trees and thick grass that concealed him from view.

Yeong-dae wanted to go to the home of Mr. Choi, the old Joseonjok man. Once there, he could find out where Nam-sik had gone. But the village that he reached was a strange and unfamiliar place. While he was crossing, it seemed, the current had swept him further down the river than he'd thought.

Yeong-dae climbed a hill some distance from the village

and watched to see if the people living there were Joseonjok or Han Chinese. Before long, he noticed Chinese police officers moving through the village. He was afraid of getting nabbed by the police if he went up to some random house. He wasn't about to let himself get caught as he had in Wangqing.

By now, Yeong-dae had run out of things to eat, and he was ravenous. He'd heard that it was possible to get by as a *kkotjebi* in downtown Yanji, but the thought of trying to find that city all by himself was overwhelming.

Staying out of sight, Yeong-dae went further into the woods and walked through a secluded area. He walked until his legs hurt, sat down to rest and massage his tired legs, and then got up again and went on. When he came across some kudzu vine, he tore off the tender shoots and ate them. He had to keep his stomach full somehow. He walked all day long, but he failed to find the village where he and Nam-sik had gone before.

What if I get lost? Where on earth could Mr. Choi's house be?

To Yeong-dae's dismay, the sun was already low on the western horizon. The sky and wind were the same as they'd always been, but Yeong-dae felt like he was all alone in the world. Without Nam-sik, he felt an empty space inside. When they'd been together, Yeong-dae hadn't been afraid to walk in the dark, but now that he was alone, he was terrified by the very idea. He had to find somewhere to sleep before it got dark.

Yeong-dae climbed a small rise a short way from the main road. He liked it because it gave him a vantage point on the village below. He also had a clear view of the road. There was a huge rock at the top of the hill, and he figured that he could hide behind the rock and get some sleep there.

After setting down his backpack, the boy started scooping up leaves piled on the slope of the hill below the rock. He was planning to lay them on the ground as bedding. As he was spreading the leaves, he suddenly came upon a row of big branches lying on the slope of the hill, pointing up to the rock above. A chill ran down his spine. When he tugged on one of the branches, it came up easily. Yeong-dae slowly pushed all of the branches to the side. Behind them was the entrance to a cave. Inside, it was pitch-black. Hurriedly, he ran to hide behind the rock.

The People in the Cave

What was in the cave? Judging by the branches hiding the entrance, it seemed obvious that people had been using it. Could it be a sentry station where Chinese police officers hid, waiting for North Korean defectors? Yeong-dae waited behind the rock and stayed perfectly still. If he didn't keep his cool, he could be in some serious trouble.

Without moving an inch, Yeong-dae listened to what was happening in the cave. He could hear faint sounds from inside. He was starting to feel nervous.

When it grew dark, the cave became quiet once more. Yeong-dae moved stealthily closer to the cave. He crept right up to the entrance. Maybe creatures of the forest were living in the cave.

His muscles tensed. What if some wild animal leaped out of the cave and attacked him?

After crouching outside the cave for some time, he carefully moved back behind the rock and hid again. It was very cold outside, but Yeong-dae was taken by an overpowering drowsiness. He couldn't keep his eyes open and soon dozed off.

A short time later, he woke up to a rustling sound, and his eyes snapped open. Right in front of him, a dark shape was moving around. He'd heard that the eyes of tigers and wolves shone in the dark. Considering that he couldn't see any glow, he guessed that this must be a person. Yeong-dae breathed as softly as he could, keeping his eyes on the black figure.

The figure stopped moving, and then there was the sound of liquid splattering on the ground. It sounded like someone was peeing. The figure was still standing up, so he guessed it was a man. A short time later, another figure emerged from the cave. This person moved a little way from the cave and then seemed to squat down. Once more, Yeong-dae heard the tinkle of water on the ground. It was the sound of a woman urinating. He realized that a man and woman were hiding in the cave. The woman moved back toward the cave.

"Ah, it feels great to be outside," said the standing figure. "I thought I was going to suffocate in there. Mom, what if the police find out we're here?"

Yeong-dae was relieved to hear someone speaking Korean. From his voice, he could tell that it was a young boy and that the woman must be his mother. Hearing the word "Mom" after so long made Yeong-dae feel a twinge of emotion. He wondered why the mother and her son were hiding in the cave. Seeing as they were North Koreans worried about the Chinese police, they were most likely defectors.

As Yeong-dae's tense muscles relaxed, his throat started to tickle. He felt a cough coming on. He held his breath to keep from coughing, but he couldn't hold it forever. At last, he released the breath that he'd been holding and coughed loudly. The woman jumped with fright.

"Who . . . who are you?" she screamed.

"I crossed the river," Yeong-dae hurriedly replied. "Can you help me?"

Neither the woman nor her son said anything in response.

"I crossed the river by myself," Yeong-dae said again, pleading with the woman.

"How did you find this place?" the woman answered at last, speaking quickly.

"I was planning on spending the night hidden behind the rock, and then I heard the sound of people."

"Did anyone see you?"

"No, they didn't. I'm by myself," Yeong-dae told her.

At last, the woman appeared to relax a little.

"Come on inside, then," she told him.

Yeong-dae followed the two into the cave. Once they were inside, the woman's son stuck the tree branches in the ground once more outside the entrance. After stumbling down a pitch-black passage, Yeong-dae saw the flickering light of a candle.

There was one more person inside, a little girl. There were three of them, all part of the same family, it seemed. In the candlelight, the boy appeared to be a couple years younger than Yeong-dae.

"I thought you were a grown-up, but you're just a few years older than my son Cheol-min," the woman said as she looked him over. "When did you cross the river?"

"It's been two days now," Yeong-dae said.

"Did you come by yourself? Where's your family?"

Reminded of his family, Yeong-dae couldn't answer for a moment.

"All of them are dead," he said at last, "except for my older sister. She's working at a hairdresser's in Shenyang. I crossed the river to find her."

The woman clucked her tongue in sympathy. The interior of the cave was dimly illuminated by the candlelight. Outside, the air was cold, but inside, it was warm and damp.

"Did you have anything to eat?" the woman said, looking at Yeong-dae. "We have a little corn flour. Would you like some?"

Yeong-dae nodded his head eagerly. The woman stirred some corn flour in water and gave it to him.

"Here's something for you to eat. We only leave the cave at night. During the day, we can't go anywhere. They say there are more police around here than there used to be. But anyhow, how are you planning to get to Shenyang all by yourself? Do you have any money?"

"One way or another, I'm going to find my sister," Yeong-dae said. "I'm worried about all of the police, though. When did you cross the river?"

"We crossed the river three days ago. We're waiting here for the person who's supposed to pick us up. They'll probably be here tomorrow," she said.

Yeong-dae wondered how they could have endured three whole days in the cave. He had many questions to ask her.

"Where are they going to take you? Is this cave safe? How did you find out about the cave?"

"We're going to South Korea," the woman said. "The cave is safe. The person who helped us cross the river brought us here. We were told that a lot of defectors from the Republic stay here for a few days. The missionary said he'd be coming to pick us up tomorrow night, so right now we're waiting for him."

Yeong-dae was surprised to hear that someone had helped them cross the river.

"The person who helped you cross the river?" he repeated, with curiosity in his voice.

"There are people who have an agreement with the border guards. If you give them money, they help you cross the river."

Yeong-dae couldn't believe his ears.

"Are you saying the border guards actually *help* people cross the river?"

The woman explained to Yeong-dae how brokers collected money from their clients and then paid the border guards to help their clients make it across the river. While the soldiers were certainly supposed to be guarding the border, they took bribes when their superiors weren't watching and told people when there wouldn't be a patrol. And when the guards were on duty, they'd sometimes fire their guns in the air, too. The gunfire that Yeong-dae had heard might have been something of this sort. To Yeong-dae, it sounded like his country was little more than a joke.

"If you go to South Korea, you can live a good life, too," the woman was telling Yeong-dae. "My husband already went to South Korea. He used his resettlement money to pay a broker to bring us to him. If we'd stayed in the Republic, we might have starved to death."

Yeong-dae already knew that South Koreans had good lives, and he wanted to go there as well. But finding his older sister came first.

"I have to find my sister," Yeong-dae said. "After that, I'll think about going to South Korea."

"You said she was in Shenyang, didn't you?" the woman asked. "When Mr. Park gets here tomorrow, you should ask him how to get there."

Yeong-dae was surprised to hear that the missionary's name was Mr. Park. Mr. Choi the acupuncturist had mentioned a missionary named Mr. Park. Could it be the same person? If it was, Yeong-dae might be able to find out what had happened to Nam-sik. That was an exciting thought.

As Yeong-dae relaxed, he felt drowsy. Soon, he drifted off to sleep.

When he opened his eyes the next day, he could see sunlight filtering into the cave. The entrance was blocked by tree branches, just as when Yeong-dae had first found it. From the outside, a passerby would never have guessed anything was there.

"During the day, you must be sure not to go outside," the woman said when she saw Yeong-dae peering outside. "Tonight, the missionary is going to come get us. We have to stay here and wait until then."

Yeong-dae took the edge off his appetite with a simple meal of corn. He stayed in the cave all day long. He was jealous of the younger boy Cheol-min. His parents were still alive, and he was going to South Korea.

The day dragged on and on, and Yeong-dae had trouble suppressing the urge to go outside. As the day grew dark, the four of them started getting excited. Each gust of wind made them think that Mr. Park had come to pick them up. With nervous anticipation, they waited as one hour and then another hour slipped by.

By the middle of the night, though, they felt anxious. Had

Mr. Park been arrested by the police? The woman worried whether the broker had been lying to them. The four of them sat near the entrance to the cave in the dark, waiting for the missionary. They waited all night, but he didn't show up.

The next day, the woman was frantic. She said they were running out of food. Mr. Park didn't move during the daytime because it was too dangerous, so she decided she and her children would wait one more night.

Yeong-dae made up his mind to wait one more day, too. If Mr. Park still didn't show up, he'd just have to set out on his own. He wanted to find Mr. Choi if he could and ask what had happened to Nam-sik.

Lunch passed and then supper, and the group's nerves were on edge. After the sun went down, the four of them left the cave. After carefully putting the branches back in place, they hid behind the rock and waited for Mr. Park.

Around dusk, a man dressed like a woodcutter turned off the main road and came trudging up the hill. The stranger gradually got closer, but the four people behind the rock didn't move. The woman whispered to the children that it might not be Mr. Park. She told them not to reveal their location until they were sure who he was.

When the stranger reached the entrance to the cave, he glanced around and then pushed the branches to the side. He stuck his head into the cave and said in a low voice, "Is anyone there? This is Mr. Park."

The woman scrambled out from behind the rock at once.

"Mr. Park! We're over here. You're Mr. Park the missionary, right?"

"Why are you outside of the cave? Hurry inside!"

The five of them entered the cave, and the woman lit the candle. Mr. Park opened his backpack and pulled out a smaller sack.

"I was told there would be three of you altogether, but it looks like there are four here," Mr. Park said as he looked them over.

The woman told him that Yeong-dae hadn't been part of the group but had crossed the river by himself.

"That explains that," Mr. Park said. "But before we go any further, let's have a bite to eat. I bet you're quite hungry. I'm sorry about being late. I was delayed by circumstances beyond my control."

Mr. Park took bread and dumplings out of the sack and handed them out. Yeong-dae couldn't believe how good they tasted. It was the best food he'd eaten since being at Mr. Choi's house.

Mr. Park asked Yeong-dae various questions and listened attentively to the boy's answers.

"Shenyang is a busy city," Mr. Park said when he'd heard the whole story. "There are a lot of North Korean defectors, a lot of regular Chinese people, and a lot of Chinese police officers. There are also quite a few North Korean spies, of course. For that reason, it's a dangerous place to be."

Yeong-dae wanted to find out what had happened to Nam-sik.

"Mr. Park," he said, "do you by any chance know an old Joseonjok man living in Helong who's good at acupuncture?"

An expression of surprise crossed Mr. Park's face for a moment.

"You mean the old man whose son and daughter-in-law both went to South Korea? The man whose house is at the bottom of the hill?"

Yeong-dae's heart turned a somersault.

"Yes, sir. That's who I mean. Do you know him?"

"You bet I do! He's helped a lot of North Koreans."

"So in that case, I guess you must be that missionary he was talking about!"

Yeong-dae was so eager to learn the truth that he couldn't stop asking questions. Mr. Park was surprised to hear that Yeong-dae knew the acupuncturist.

"How do you know that old man?" Mr. Park asked.

Just thinking about Nam-sik was painful for Yeong-dae. While he was telling Mr. Park everything that had happened, he had to keep wiping away the tears forming in his eyes.

"Ah," Mr. Park said with a nod. "So you're the boy that got caught trying to find his sister!"

"Yes, that's me. What happened to Nam-sik?"

Mr. Park shook his head slowly and sighed.

"When I got to Mr. Choi's house, Nam-sik had already left. I'd run into some trouble, too, and I lost a lot of time hiding from the police. I ended up getting to Mr. Choi's house a week later than planned. After your arrest, I learned that the police searched the area with a fine-toothed comb. Mr. Choi told me that Nam-sik left, worried that his presence there might put the Choi family in danger.

"When Nam-sik left, Mr. Choi gave him my phone number, but I never heard from him. I hope he made it to South Korea safely, but there's no way to know. Mr. Choi was really worried about you, too."

Yeong-dae was crushed to hear that Mr. Park didn't know where Nam-sik was. But the missionary was already asking him another question.

"What a remarkable coincidence this all is. Anyway, you were taken to North Korea and then escaped once again, I guess?"

"That's right," Yeong-dae said. "My older sister's in Shenyang, and I'm determined to find her. But if Shenyang is such a dangerous place, what should I do?"

Mr. Park mulled the question over for a while and then asked one of his own.

"Women can stay hidden in massage parlors, beauty parlors, bathhouses, and other places, but it might be a dangerous place for men. Do you know the address where your sister's living?"

Yeong-dae shook his head. If he didn't even know the address, Mr. Park asked worriedly, was he planning to visit every beauty parlor in Shenyang? If he had to, Yeong-dae thought, that's exactly what he'd to. He was going to find his sister even if that meant going through every nook and cranny in Shenyang.

"So what should I do? Can you help me?" Yeong-dae asked.

"Yes, I can. But first, we're leaving here at 4 o'clock in the morning. For now, you can come with us. We'll work out the details on the way."

The car was going to pick them up the following morning, Mr. Park said, so they should pack their things now. The woman tidied up the cave where she and her children had slept for the past few days and bustled around, getting ready for the long journey. Yeong-dae had trouble getting to sleep as he thought about Nam-sik.

When I find my sister, I really want to go live in South Korea. Maybe I can meet Nam-sik there. I wonder what in the world happened to him . . .

Yeong-dae went to the entrance to the cave and peered between the branches, up at the black night sky. On some star way up in the heavens, he thought, maybe his mother, father, and little sister were looking down at him.

If only he'd been born in some other country, Yeong-dae and his family might have lived together happily. He would have gone to the ends of the Earth to find his parents and little sister, but he knew that no amount of traveling could bring them back again. The thought that he'd never see his family again made him cry. He missed his friend Nam-sik as well.

As Yeong-dae was wiping away his tears, Mr. Park came up

behind him.

"I know the owner of a Joseonjok restaurant in Shenyang," the missionary said. "The restaurant owner and his wife help North Korean refugees. If you go to the city with the vague idea of finding your sister and no specific plans, you'll be in trouble because you won't have a place to stay. You don't know for sure where your sister is, either. Let me try asking the restaurant owner to let you stay at the restaurant and work there. You can look for your sister in your free time."

Yeong-dae didn't know how to say how thankful he felt. It was as if a brilliant light had suddenly appeared in the darkest hour of the night. He didn't sleep a wink that night. As the group left the cave, they erased their footprints and then buried their trash in the ground to hide all signs that people had stayed there. The vehicle that was coming to pick them up could only go as far as Yanji. From there, Mr. Park said, they'd have to board a night bus while keeping a sharp eye out for the police.

Mr. Park turned over a small rock in front of the mouth of the cave and stuck a branch shaped like a slingshot into the ground right in front of it.

"This is a signal for the people who help defectors cross the river. It lets them know that we left safely. All right! Let's get a move on," he said.

Yeong-dae realized that the cave would serve as a temporary shelter for others who would cross the river, leaving North Korea behind.

Mr. Park took the lead. At a curve in the road, there was a large pine tree. As soon as the car stopped in front of that tree, Mr. Park said, they had to jump in and get going. The five of them went past the pine tree, crouched down in the ditch next to the road, and waited for the vehicle to arrive.

"After the sun comes up, you never know when the police will drive by," Mr. Park said. "The van can't stop for long. When it gets here, everyone has to get in just as soon as I give the word."

Before long, they finally heard the sound of a vehicle. Since it was coming from around the bend, they couldn't see it. Mr. Park told them not to climb out of the ditch until they were sure it wasn't a police car. They all waited without moving until the vehicle came closer. Finally, it appeared.

"That's it!" Mr. Park shouted. "Hurry and get in!"

As soon as the van stopped, the door swung open. The van waited with its engine humming while Yeong-dae and the other four sprinted toward it and jumped inside. They ran as fast as a deer being chased by a tiger. The van took off even before the door had shut. Mr. Park turned around and watched the road behind them to make sure that there weren't any cars back there. When they were sure no one was tailing them, everyone in the vehicle let out a big sigh of relief. Mr. Park pulled out a bundle from beneath his seat. It was full of used clothing.

"Okay, hurry and change your clothes," Mr. Park said. "If the Chinese authorities question us, you have to look Chinese."

Mr. Park told them to change into neat clothing and straighten up their hair to get rid of any signs that they had been staying in a cave. He even pulled out some used pairs of tennis shoes that he had gotten somewhere and had them select the pairs that were the best fit. The shoes that Yeong-dae was given were a little big for him, but they were still much better than the shoes he had been wearing. The woman combed her daughter's hair and then her own.

The driver of the van seemed to be Chinese, as Mr. Park was speaking to him in that language. When a car passed by in the opposite lane, everyone in the van tried to look as bored as possible. If they were to make it to South Korea, they had to safely reach Kunming, a border city in southern China. Mr. Park said it could take several days to get there.

Mr. Park made frequent phone calls to all kinds of people. Seeing him on the phone made Yeong-dae nervous. It reminded him of the Chinese man who called the police to report him.

"When the van stops, be sure not to gawk," Mr. Park told them. If you do, people will see in an instant that you're a defector. You have to act very nonchalant. The safest bet is pretending to be asleep."

The four defectors nodded their heads solemnly, their faces full of fear. After driving for a while, the little girl started feeling nauseous, so Mr. Park handed her a plastic bag. When the driver stopped the van to fill the tank with gas, Mr. Park got out and came back with some bread, which they had for lunch.

They kept driving all day and finally reached Yanji around dusk. As soon as they got out of the van, the missionary whisked them into an alley and then into a run-down eatery. They ate a simple dinner and then boarded a night bus headed for Shenyang. Yeong-dae could hardly believe that he was going to Shenyang, the city his sister was supposedly living in.

As soon as Yeong-dae sat down in his seat, he fell right asleep. When he opened his eyes, it was the next morning.

Yeong-dae rubbed his eyes and looked out the window.

"We're in Shenyang," Mr. Park told him.

"Huh? We're already here?"

"That's right! The other three and I have to transfer to another bus here. I wish I could go with you to the restaurant I told you about, but it would be dangerous for the whole group to move together. You'll have to find it by yourself. I'll call ahead and let them know you're coming."

Mr. Park handed Yeong-dae a map he had drawn and then continued.

"Here's my phone number. The nature of my work means I can't stay in the same place for long, but I can usually answer the phone. If you need any help, give me a call on this number. I hope that you find your sister. Oh, and this is for you."

Mr. Park pressed some money into Yeong-dae's hand.

"No, I can't take the money, Mr. Park," Yeong-dae said, shaking his head. "I'm incredibly thankful just for you helping me to get here in one piece. Oh, I do have a favor to ask you. If you hear from my friend Nam-sik, can you please tell me where he is? I have to find him."

Yeong-dae really didn't want to take the missionary's money. More accurately, he didn't feel like he deserved it.

"It's risky not having any money here," Mr. Park told him. "When you're on the run from the police, you might need to take a taxi, and if you need to hole up somewhere, you'll need to pay for a room. Going around and begging like a *kkotjebi* would be even more dangerous. No protests, Yeong-dae. Put the money in your pocket."

Yeong-dae felt so thankful that he started crying. The rest of the group said their goodbyes quickly as they had no time to lose. Now, Yeong-dae would have to find the restaurant that Mr. Park had told him about all by himself.

Barbecued Ribs in Shenyang

The Joseonjok restaurant that Mr. Park had told Yeong-dae about was called Suwon Barbecued Ribs. The restaurant was located on Tumen Street in Xita, a Shenyang district largely populated by ethnic Koreans. Yeong-dae had Mr. Park's map in his hand when he got to Xita. Shenyang was a forest of tall buildings that reminded Yeong-dae of the rows of pine trees lining the slopes of Mount Baekdu.

His stomach was rumbling, so he followed the mouth-watering aromas in the air toward a nearby market bustling with people. His appetite was piqued by the savory smell of lamb on the grill. Dozens of people were talking in loud voices, trying to be heard over the roar, and Yeong-dae's ears were soon ringing. The market seemed even noisier because Korean and Chinese conversations were all jumbled together. Yeong-dae bought some pita bread as a snack, as it was the cheapest thing he could find. The bread looked huge, but when he bit into it, he learned that there was nothing but air beneath the bulging crust.

Most of the store signs in Shenyang were written in Chinese characters with Korean letters underneath. The neighborhood of Xita—meaning "Western Pavilion"—included the pavilion itself and a grid made of the streets of Xita, Fushun, Hunchun, Tumen, and Shifu, all located to the east of the pavilion. Yeong-dae headed to Tumen Street first. Whenever he saw the word "beauty parlor" on a sign, his heart skipped a beat. If he ran right in, could he find his sister? Yeong-dae knew that if he was too hasty, he might not only fail to find his sister but could also be arrested again by the Chinese police.

Yeong-dae moved east along Xita Street, keeping an eye on signs on both sides of the road as he went. Signs in Korean were hanging everywhere on the sides of the buildings. He saw "Morangwan Hall," "Gyeongbokgung Palace," and a photo studio. There were so many signs that Yeong-dae felt as if he'd stepped into a strange new world. He'd seen nothing like this in North Korea.

Whenever Yeong-dae saw anyone dressed like a police officer, he'd duck into an alleyway. After a while, he reached Tumen Street, where he noticed signs saying "Pearl Karaoke" and "Our Seoul." But no matter where he turned, he couldn't see a sign for Suwon Barbecued Ribs.

He kept following the road, assuming that he was still on Tumen Street, but suddenly he saw a sign that said "Hunchun Street." Once again, he pulled out the map that Mr. Park had drawn for him. Figuring it might attract attention to open up the map in the middle of the street, he found a quiet section of the sidewalk and unfolded the map there. Suwon Barbecued Ribs was definitely located on Tumen Street. He saw that Hunchun Street picked up where Tumen Street came to an end.

Following the instructions on the map, Yeong-dae walked back the way he had come, looking all around for the restaurant. He caught sight of Do-Re-Mi Bathhouse. That was on the map, but he hadn't noticed it before. *That's the ticket,* Yeong-dae thought, feeling a sense of relief. *I'm on the right track.*

Now he was more alert, peering carefully at each sign that

he passed. He walked past a cluster of signs written only in Chinese. Thinking he'd lost his way again, Yeong-dae slipped into an alley and opened up the map yet again. Sure enough, Suwon Barbecued Ribs was in the same alley as Do-Re-Mi Bathhouse.

Yeong-dae retraced his steps once more. Finally he saw it—a signboard that said "Suwon Barbecued Ribs" in red letters. The map showed a store called "Coco's Supermarket" next to the restaurant, and Yeong-dae could see that, too. He had no idea what a supermarket was, but the important thing was that he'd found the restaurant.

When Yeong-dae got to Suwon Barbecued Ribs, it was evening. The area in front of the restaurant was bustling with people. He made his way through the crowd and slipped inside.

As Yeong-dae looked around the inside of the restaurant, he saw a big woman sitting behind the cash register. He suddenly wished he'd asked Mr. Park what the owner of the restaurant looked like. As Yeong-dae stood hesitantly next to the counter, the woman gazed at him intently and then motioned for him to come closer.

"Would you happen to be the boy that Mr. Park told us was

coming?" she asked.

Yeong-dae nodded eagerly, and the woman stood up and came out from behind the counter. She called over a woman with a ponytail to watch the register, and then led Yeong-dae toward the kitchen. As he walked behind her, he gazed curiously around the restaurant. He saw groups of people sitting around circular aluminum tables. In the hollow place in the middle of each table was a large iron pot filled with coals, and on top of that was a round wire grill covered with chunks of sizzling meat.

Next to the kitchen was a narrow hallway that ended in a small closet. When the woman opened the closet door, Yeong-dae saw a room littered with various containers of spices, seat cushions, and aprons. It was barely big enough for two people to lie down on the floor side by side.

"Go on in," the big woman told him. "I heard all about you from Mr. Park. Wait here until I get back."

The woman, Yeong-dae learned, was married to the restaurant's owner. Her name was Mrs. Kang. He nervously wondered what kind of work he would have to do. While he was waiting for the woman to return, he felt a sudden urge to run outside and go looking for beauty parlors.

Four years had passed since Yeong-dae had last seen his sister Yeong-ran. He fondly remembered how she'd run her fingers through her hair the night before she left the house. He wanted to smell the fragrance of her hair. When he saw his sister, what would he tell her first? She was probably living on the run, too. As he waited in the tiny closet, dozens of thoughts ran through his head. After quite a while, Mrs. Kang opened the door.

"You can come out, now," she told him.

Yeong-dae quickly followed the woman out of the closet. She led him into the kitchen. She handed him rubber kitchen gloves and told him to clean the wire grills soaking in a big tub nearby. The grills were black and sticky from charred meat and marinade.

Everyone in the kitchen moved in a tremendous hurry. One person was loading trays with side dishes, another was doing the dishes, and a third was chopping up the meat. Mrs. Kang gave Yeong-dae a wire brush.

"You can clean the grills with this," she said. "Do you think you can handle this?"

Nodding his head, Yeong-dae squatted down and started scrubbing the wire grills in the tub. Servers kept bringing him more sticky grills to wash from the dining area. He wondered what barbecued beef ribs tasted like. As he counted the number of grills, Yeong-dae imagined just how many customers were eating barbecue in the restaurant.

After a while, the noisy restaurant began to grow quiet. Servers were no longer tossing dirty grills into the tub. When Yeong-dae finished cleaning the last grill, he tried to get up, but he could barely make it to his feet. His legs had nearly fallen asleep during the several hours he had spent squatting on the floor and scraping off grills.

Not a single customer remained in the restaurant. The cooks were in the kitchen making some dinner for the rest of the staff. That was when Yeong-dae realized just how famished he was. He'd been so focused on his work that he hadn't had a chance to think about anything else. Before they dug in to the food, Mrs. Kang introduced Yeong-dae to the rest of the workers.

"This boy will be working in the kitchen with us from now on. Greet your new co-workers, Yeong-dae."

Yeong-dae bowed his head in a respectful greeting. Since all of the workers were Joseonjok who spoke Korean, he felt at ease. He'd never eaten barbecued beef ribs before, and he wasn't used to food that tasted this sweet. This was the first meat he'd eaten in a long time, and it gave him new energy. After the rest of the employees went home, the owner's wife turned to Yeong-dae.

"So I hear that you're looking for your sister," she said.

Yeong-dae nodded his head. Mrs. Kang asked him a number of questions about his sister: how old she was, how tall she was, and when she'd come to China. After answering her questions, Yeong-dae added that his sister's name was Yeong-ran and described what her face looked like.

The woman said, "Her name won't be of any help around here. There are a lot of defectors in Shenyang, and all of them are in hiding, using false names and concealing their identity. No one knows their real names. You said you're from Kilju, didn't you? I'll talk to some people at the hairdresser's that I go to. The ladies there probably have a general idea of who's working at each beauty parlor."

Mrs. Kang was very kind to Yeong-dae. Starting that day, he moved into the closet, which he shared with a teenager named Cheol-i, who was five years older than him. Cheol-i, it turned out, was doing some odd jobs at the barbecue restaurant to save up some money.

"I'm going to go to South Korea," Cheol-i told him. "If I

work for just two more years, I'll have enough money to cover airfare to South Korea and my travel expenses. My dream is to visit South Korea."

Yeong-dae was reminded of what Mr. Choi had told him about young Chinese who were struck with the "Korea bug." It looked like Cheol-i was one of them.

If it had been up to Yeong-dae, he wouldn't have wasted a single moment to look for his sister. He would have gone to every last hairdresser's shop in Xita if that's what it took. For several days, though, Mrs. Kang didn't say anything further about his sister.

Yeong-dae spent the greater part of each day scrubbing dirty wire grills. Sometimes, a few black hunks of meat were left on the grill. When Yeong-dae saw the meat that customers hadn't finished, he thought of his time as a *kkotjebi*. Even a few leftover pieces of meat would have been enough to save his little sister's life. Sometimes when he was scrubbing the grills, tears came to his eyes as he thought of Yeong-ok and his mother.

What had happened to Nam-sik? Yeong-dae figured that Nam-sik had probably been arrested and taken back to North Korea. He missed Nam-sik as much as he missed Yeong-ran.

Sometime after Yeong-dae arrived at Suwon Barbecued Ribs, Yeong-dae and Cheol-i were given a day off, and Mrs. Kang told Cheol-i to take the boy out and show him around the neighborhood. Yeong-dae was filled with excitement at the thought of touring the beauty parlors in the area.

But since it was a day off, Cheol-i slept in quite late. Yeong-dae wanted to be out of the house so badly that he could barely keep still. Suspecting that Yeong-dae might feel that way, Mrs. Kang had told him in no uncertain terms that he mustn't go outside by himself. She told him that he'd be running the risk of getting caught by the police, and that if he *did* get caught, the restaurant would have to pay a fine, too. She made it clear that, if Yeong-dae wanted to go out, he'd have to go out with Cheol-i.

Yeong-dae waited impatiently for Cheol-i to get up. Time crawled, as slow as a snail.

A Tour of Xita

Cheol-i didn't get up until after lunchtime. Apparently unaware of how badly Yeong-dae wanted to get going, Cheol-i ate a leisurely lunch and took a long shower. After that, he spent quite a while getting his hair ready. He kept changing his mind about the hair gel, rubbing in one kind and then washing it out again. Once he settled on a gel, it took him even longer to arrange his hair. Standing in front of the mirror, he combed it up and then back down again.

Next, Cheol-i had to choose his clothes. He tried on one outfit after the other until Yeong-dae was so frustrated that he couldn't bear watching anymore. If Cheol-i only had one pair of clothes, like Yeong-dae, he could get dressed in no time.

Having so many clothes meant there were a lot of decisions to make. It was the same with the older boy's shoes. Cheol-i said they had to match his outfit. He showed each pair of shoes to Yeong-dae, one after the other, and asked him whether they looked good with what he was wearing.

To Yeong-dae, Cheol-i's attempt to look fashionable seemed immature. If Cheol-i was really saving up money to go to South Korea, why did he try so hard to look cool when he went out to meet his friends? Yeong-dae was in such a hurry to go out that he told Cheol-i that he looked fine no matter what the older boy asked him.

At last, the two of them left the barbecue restaurant. Yeong-dae couldn't wait to visit the beauty parlors. But just then, Cheol-i remembered that he'd left his mobile phone inside and went back into the restaurant. When he returned, he had not just his phone but also a baseball cap, which he put on Yeong-dae's head.

"You need to wear this cap, Yeong-dae," Cheol-i said. "Something about your hair looks awkward, and the police officers here have sharp eyes. This cap may be fake, but it still says 'GAP' on it."

Yeong-dae was a little uncomfortable about having English

letters on the cap — since it was from America — but he felt much safer now that he was wearing it. He'd been mad at Cheol-i because of how slowly he got dressed, but when Yeong-dae got to wear the hat, his anger vanished and he felt grateful instead.

Yeong-dae walked behind Cheol-i and kept an eye out for beauty parlor billboards. As they weaved their way through the press of people, Yeong-dae kept close to the older boy, afraid that he might lose him in the crowd.

After walking toward the middle of Xita, Cheol-i turned into an alley across from Hunchun Street.

"This is where most of the hairdressers are. There are tons of massage parlors, beauty parlors, and bathhouses around here," he told Yeong-dae as they entered the alley.

Signboards advertising the various businesses were hung all over the building walls. To Yeong-dae, all of the businesses were unfamiliar. He saw Wangcho Gentleman's Club, Gaseong Salon, and Ain Beautician. As Yeong-dae read the signs, he glanced around, wondering why there weren't any signs for beauty parlors.

"But where are all the hairdressers?" Yeong-dae asked Cheol-i in confusion.

"We just passed a few right there. Didn't you see them?"

Taken aback, Yeong-dae came to a halt and stared at Cheol-i blankly, shaking his head.

"Can't you read? It says 'salon' right over there!"

Cheol-i was staring at Yeong-dae in surprise and pity.

"What's a salon?" Yeong-dae said. "I don't know what that means."

"Ah, you must not use that word in North Korea! A salon is the same as a beauty parlor. I guess you just didn't know the meaning of the word."

Cheol-i nodded his head to show that he understood. That was when Yeong-dae learned that a salon is the same thing as a beauty parlor. He wondered whether Yeong-ran was really working in one of the shops that said "salon." He wanted to go in then and there and look for her.

Cheol-i might have had some idea of what Yeong-dae was thinking, because he said, "Today, we're just going around to get a general idea of where the hairdressers are located. Running in and saying you're looking for your sister would be nearly as bad as walking up to a cop and saying, 'Arrest me! I'm a defector.'"

Yeong-dae's spirits had been high, but now they started to

sink. Noticing Yeong-dae's discouragement, Cheol-i went on.

"Your sister didn't have enough money to set up her own shop, right? That means she's working for someone else, and so she has to hide the fact that she's a North Korean defector. If you suddenly burst into a shop, you'll be putting not only yourself at risk, but your sister as well. That's why you can't rush things, OK?"

Yeong-dae was pouting and didn't answer.

"You can't expect everything to happen at once," Cheol-i said, trying to make him feel better. "Mrs. Kang is probably making some quiet inquiries. All we can do is wait. We don't know what's going to happen, or when. Try to think of today as a chance to tour Xita and check out a few places."

That wasn't what Yeong-dae wanted to hear, but he completely understood what the older boy was saying. Yeong-dae had been foolish to think that he'd find his sister as soon as he got to Shenyang. In fact, it was an incredible piece of luck that Mr. Park had found him a place to stay at the barbecue restaurant, where he could eat and sleep in safety.

The first time Yeong-dae crossed the river into China, he'd been caught because he'd acted rashly without taking any precautions. This time around, he really needed to be more careful.

As Cheol-i and Yeong-dae walked around Xita, they saw children in rags following well-dressed men and women. "Help us!" the children yelled, "We're hungry." The scene was only too familiar to Yeong-dae. They were *kkotjebi* from North Korea who were approaching South Korean tourists at the night market and begging. Why didn't the Chinese police try to catch the *kkotjebi*?

Seeing the beggar children made Yeong-dae feel ashamed to be from North Korea. He was sad to have been born in a country that lied to its own people. North Koreans were told that their country was heaven on earth, and their government had even invented its own holiday, the Sun Festival[15]. It was hard for Yeong-dae to believe that he'd once felt proud and happy to have been born there. It made him angry to think of his poor starving people who, despite not having enough to eat, kept honoring the Great Leader as if he were the sun itself.

"Those *kkotjebi* come running as soon as they see a South Korean," Cheol-i muttered as he looked at the children.

"Why is that?"

---

15. The Sun Festival is the day when North Koreans celebrate the birthday of Kim Il-sung, founder of the country.

"South Korean tourists give them food and money because they feel sorry for them."

"Are there a lot of South Korean tourists here?" Yeong-dae asked.

"Sure there are! There are a lot of tourists from South Korea, but there are also quite a few South Koreans who come to Shenyang to open up businesses. South Korea is an amazing country. Even here in Shenyang, nearly all of the big stores are run by South Koreans. That's why they say that Shenyang is like a little piece of South Korea inside China."

This took Yeong-dae by surprise. He already knew that South Korea was better off than North Korea. If South Korea was even richer than the amazing city of Shenyang, he thought, it truly must be an amazing place.

At that moment, a group of white tourists walked past Yeong-dae. He stared at them for some time. He guessed that they must be Americans.

"What are you looking at?" Cheol-i finally asked him.

"Cheol-i, how do you feel when you see Americans? Don't they scare you?"

Cheol-i seemed puzzled by Yeong-dae's question.

"What would I be scared of? They're not scary at all. What

do you mean?"

"When I was younger, I thought that Americans were scary-looking monsters with horns coming out of their heads," Yeong-dae said. "I was taught that they were our mortal enemies."

Hearing this, Cheol-i smiled.

"Americans help the *kkotjebi* a lot, too," he said. "They're definitely not monsters."

Yeong-dae couldn't take his eyes off the American tourists until they were out of sight.

The two boys wandered through Xita until late that night. Bright lights came on, illuminating the signboards, and the area looked even more exciting than it had in the daylight.

Yeong-dae had never seen a city as splendid as this one. It felt like a totally different world from North Korea. His country went dark when the sun went down because there wasn't enough electricity to keep the lights on.

Where could my sister be? Did she think I'd come looking for her?

That night, in Yeong-dae's dreams, he wandered around in search of his sister until he woke up.

The next day, Yeong-dae went back to scrubbing the wire

grills. He gradually got the hang of it, and the work became easier than it had been at first. For the first few days, his arms had hurt, but after ten days on the job, it was no longer a big deal.

Yeong-dae walked around the Xita area several times by himself. He no longer got lost even when he was alone. He tried to finish doing the dishes after supper as fast as possible so that he could spend more time watching the hairdressers getting off work. Each morning, he wrapped up his chores quickly and then asked Mrs. Kang if he could go watch the hairdressers on their way to work. He'd heard that most beauty parlors didn't open for business until after 10 in the morning.

Every day, Yeong-dae watched a different beauty parlor. One evening, he even trailed a woman who looked a little like his sister. Yeong-dae was sorry that he couldn't visit all of the beauty parlors in Shenyang.

While working at Suwon Barbecued Ribs, Yeong-dae was given plenty to eat, and it showed. He started putting on a little weight, and his face looked healthier. The workers at the store told him that they could hardly tell he was from North Korea anymore. When the police were snooping around, Mrs. Kang would give him a signal, and he would stay hidden until they left.

Reunion

Two months after Yeong-dae arrived in Shenyang, Mrs. Kang called Yeong-dae over for a chat.

"I've been told that there's a hairdresser in town from North Korea who's the same age as your sister," the woman said. "I got in touch with her and asked her to come by when she's free. We need to meet her in private because there are things we can't ask with other people around."

Yeong-dae's face flushed with excitement, and his heart started to race.

When Mrs. Kang saw how excited he was getting, she said, "She might not be your sister, you know. But even if she's not, don't get too disappointed. When the hairdresser comes, we can ask her a lot of questions. If you're sure that your sister's really here in Shenyang, we'll find her."

Yeong-dae felt like his chest would burst with joy. Every morning and evening as he watched people streaming in and out of beauty parlors, he'd been thinking what he should say when he saw his sister and how she would've changed.

The woman whom Mrs. Kang was talking about just had to be Yeong-dae's sister! She was the same age, she was a defector, and she was a hairdresser—who else could it be, if not Yeong-ran? Yeong-dae was as excited as if he'd already found his sister.

Starting the next day, he kept his eyes glued to the customers entering the restaurant. When people came inside, he would drop the grill he was scraping and stick his head outside the kitchen to check on them. He wasn't quite sure how he made it through the day.

Mrs. Kang scolded Yeong-dae time and time again for being so distracted, but he just couldn't stay focused on his work. Even after work was over and all the employees had gone home, Yeong-dae didn't want to lock the door of the restaurant. He felt anxious that his sister would come, find the door locked, and go home again. Each day, he waited up for her until late in the evening.

She probably can't come in the daytime because she has to work then. Even after work is over, she probably moves around late at night. She wants to avoid being seen and reported to the police. Yeong-ran, hurry up!

Yeong-dae spent much of his time daydreaming about finally seeing his sister.

Ten days passed, but his sister still didn't come.

"Mrs. Kang," Yeong-dae suggested one day, "would it be OK for me to go out to find her?

He was so excited that he could barely stay in his seat.

"Let's wait a few more days and then get in touch with her again," Mrs. Kang said as she shook her head. "I'm curious about why we haven't heard anything from the woman, too, but let's be patient for a little longer."

When he heard this, Yeong-dae decided to keep waiting.

About a month later, Yeong-dae finished his work early and was looking outside through the glass door. Suddenly, he saw a young woman approaching with a scarf wrapped around her face and neck. She was nervously glancing from side to side as she made her way toward the restaurant. She was about as tall as Yeong-dae's sister, and she also had the same gait.

Yeong-dae shot out of the restaurant like a bullet. He ran straight toward the woman and then came to a stop right in front of her, nearly crashing right into her. The woman stared at Yeong-dae in surprise. His pounding heart skipped a beat.

It wasn't his sister. The woman looked around nervously and then went inside the barbecue restaurant.

Filled with disappointment, Yeong-dae followed her inside. The woman was talking with Mrs. Kang.

"Where did you go?" the owner's wife said as soon as she saw Yeong-dae. "Is the woman your sister?"

Yeong-dae shook his head, tears welling up in his eyes. Obviously confused, the woman looked back and forth between Yeong-dae and Mrs. Kang.

"At any rate, why don't you take a seat," Mrs. Kang told the other woman disappointedly. "Yeong-dae, you come join us."

The woman told them that she was there because Mrs. Kang's regular hair stylist had asked her to come, but that she didn't know what was going on. Mrs. Kang brought out some food for her to eat as they talked.

While the woman was eating, Mrs. Kang explained in detail what had happened to Yeong-dae and his sister. When she heard his story, the woman told them her own. She was from

Musan and had crossed the river five years ago. At first, she lived in hiding at the beauty parlor, cleaning the store and washing customers' hair. About a year ago, she said, she had started working as a hairdresser.

Yeong-dae described his sister in detail and begged the woman to help him find her. The woman thought for a bit and after a while spoke again.

"A woman like the one you described used to be at a salon that I know of, but the police caught her a few years ago. I heard she was taken to the Republic and then escaped once more, but I'm not sure where she went after that. I'll try to help you find her."

Yeong-dae pleaded with the woman to find out what she could about his sister. After the woman left, he went back to waiting anxiously for news.

Two months after that, the woman visited the barbecue restaurant again.

"I'm not totally sure about this," she said, "but I heard through the grapevine that the woman I told you about is working for a South Korean beauty parlor on Fushun Street."

Yeong-dae asked where Fushun Street was. He wanted to go find the beauty parlor that very moment.

"It's a little far from here," she told him. "There are quite a few beauty parlors on Antu Street, but this one is on the opposite side of the district."

After the woman finished eating, she said it was getting late and got ready to go. Thanking the woman for her help, Mrs. Kang reminded her to keep all of this a secret. Yeong-dae was about to follow the hairdresser outside, but Cheol-i stopped him.

"It's too late today, Yeong-dae," he said. "You have the day off tomorrow, so you can spend the whole day looking for her."

Yeong-dae reluctantly agreed to wait. Now that he knew that the woman had been arrested, he felt even more certain that she was his sister. Had his sister been tortured in prison after being taken back to North Korea? He'd heard that women had to undergo all kinds of horrible things in prison. There was no way that Yeong-ran could have escaped such torture. It seemed clear that she'd finally gone home after being released from a labor camp or reeducation center.

You must've been so shocked to get home and find Mother and Father dead and me and Yeong-ok gone! How painful that must've been for you.

Early the next morning, Yeong-dae put on the cap Cheol-I

had given him and headed to Fushun Street. He figured that it wouldn't be too hard to find a beauty parlor run by a South Korean if he asked around once he got to the general area.

Yeong-dae hoped that there would only be one South Korean salon on Fushun Street. What would the sign out front look like? Would it say "hairdresser?" Would it say "beautician"? Or maybe "hair salon"? Yeong-dae realized that he was learning a lot.

He saw Jinmi Pub, Hyogun Doors & Windows, Clam Noodle Soup . . . and next to that, Seoul Beauty Parlor. The sign looked South Korean to him. Since Seoul was the capital of South Korea, he figured a South Korean was running the store. Yeong-dae dashed over to the entrance, but the door was locked. He realized that it was still too early. It wasn't 10 in the morning yet.

Yeong-dae decided to wait outside the shop until it opened for the day. He hoped so badly that Yeong-ran would show up for work at Seoul Beauty Parlor. He thought of his mother, his father, and Yeong-ok.

I'm begging all of you . . . help me meet my sister today!

Yeong-dae put his hands together and prayed in front of the beauty parlor. He prayed the way he'd seen his mother pray when he was young. He felt sure that if he wanted something this badly, it would have to come true. In an instant, the things he'd experienced flashed through his mind. When his father passed away, he'd been so young. When his mother was arrested, it had happened so fast that he didn't know what to do. And when Yeong-ok had been taken from him, he had wanted to follow her to the grave.

But now, Yeong-dae was trying to find his sister and find a new kind of life. Was she making her way to the salon right now? Yeong-dae stood in front of the door and looked at each woman who walked by.

After some time had passed, he heard the door opening behind him. Someone must have unlocked the door! Spinning around with surprise, he saw the back of a woman going inside. In a flash, Yeong-dae followed her into the salon. The woman gasped with shock when she saw him.

Yeong-dae stood stock-still, his whole body trembling as if an electric current was running through him. Just in front of him was standing a stranger with a stunned expression on her face. She looked a little like the older sister Yeong-dae had missed so much, but her skin was clearer and her figure had filled out. Her eyes were definitely his sister's, but there was something unexpected about her.

"Could it . . . could it be . . .?" the woman said. She seemed as surprised as Yeong-dae. His lips were stuck together, and no words would come out.

After a pause, he finally managed to speak.

"Yeong-ran . . . it's you, isn't it? It's me, Yeong-dae."

At last, Yeong-ran overcame her shock and took Yeong-dae in her arms.

"Yeong-dae!" she said through her sobs. "You're my little Yeong-dae, aren't you? You're Yeong-dae, right?"

He wanted to call his sister's name as well, but couldn't find his voice. He could barely even breathe. He felt some great heat surging up from the depths of his soul like a river of lava. Tears gushed from his eyes like a fountain. He went limp and collapsed in his sister's arms.

"Yeong-dae . . . !" He stammered, groping for words. "Oh, I can't believe it. . . Yeong-dae!"

Brother and sister embraced each other.

"Yeong-ran! You're really Yeong-ran, aren't you? Yeong-ran, it's me! It's Yeong-dae!"

Yeong-dae couldn't keep the tears from flowing.

"I know, Yeong-dae. I know. So you're alive!"

Yeong-ran was sobbing, too. She told him that she was living in a small closet in the beauty salon. She'd gotten up early that morning, unlocked the door to the shop, and been about to start cleaning when Yeong-dae came running in.

Yeong-dae wiped away the tears and took a closer look at his sister. Her face was fairer than before, and she looked prettier, too. At the same time, he thought he saw a shadow on her face.

Working together, the two hurried to clean up the salon so they could talk before the hairdressers arrived. When they were done, Yeong-dae told his sister his story. He was sobbing the whole time, and Yeong-ran cried as she listened to him.

"I'm sorry, Yeong-dae," she told him, stroking his hand. "I'm sorry you had to endure that all by yourself. It wouldn't have been so bad if I'd been there with you."

"Yeong-ran, if our neighbor hadn't told me where you went, I wouldn't have come looking for you. I heard that you were in prison, too!"

Yeong-ran feebly nodded her head. It was heartbreaking to think that his sister had probably suffered even more than he had.

"None of that matters now," Yeong-dae said. "Now that I've found you, none of that matters. Listen, I'm not going to go back to the Republic."

"Of course! Why would anyone return to that hellhole? Now we have to create a better life for ourselves," his sister said.

Yeong-ran brushed away her tears and squeezed her lips together. After the two talked for some time, the employees at the beauty parlor began to arrive one by one. At last, a woman came in who looked to be about five or six years older than Yeong-ran.

"My little brother found me," Yeong-ran told the woman after greeting her with a bow. "Yeong-dae, bow to the lady. She's the owner here."

"Your brother?" the owner said. "You're finally back together! How did he find you?"

The owner stared at Yeong-dae with wonder in her eyes.

"You were always so weepy, but now you've found your little brother!" the owner said. "I'm so happy for you. Why don't the two of you go into your room and talk before customers start showing up? I'll call you if we get busy."

The owner seemed like a good person. Yeong-ran took her brother into the little room in the salon. It was even smaller than the closet where Yeong-dae slept in the barbecue restaurant. It was barely even big enough for one person to lie down. As soon as they entered the room, Yeong-ran massaged her brother's shoulders and sobbed some more.

"You've really grown up. You were so small when I left the house. . ."

"Yeong-ran, I hear that you've learned hairdressing? So are you a hairdresser now?"

"I learned hairdressing, but I still mostly run errands around here. But what about the place you're working at? Do they give you enough rice to eat?"

Yeong-dae could hear something sad in his sister's voice.

"Yeong-ran, not only do I have as much rice as I can eat, but I get pork ribs, too! Back in the Republic, I never dreamed of having rice and meat. Take a look at this. I've gained some weight, haven't I?"

With a big smile on his face, Yeong-dae stood up tall to show his sister how he'd grown.

"You're right," she said, nodding. "It's so easy to get rice here, but our family fell apart because we didn't have any. Mother and Father never had the chance to eat a full bowl of rice. . ."

Yeong-ran broke into sobs again, and Yeong-dae was soon crying as well.

"Yeong-ran, when I'm eating rice, sometimes I think of

Yeong-ok and I can barely get the food down."

"I can't believe that little angel starved to death. Our poor little sister . . ."

The two of them were so choked with emotion that they couldn't say anything for some time. The owner of the beauty parlor didn't call Yeong-ran all morning long. From time to time, Yeong-ran would step outside for a moment to see if there was anything she needed to do. But each time she came out of the room, the owner told her to keep talking and sent her back inside.

At lunch time, the owner even ordered some food for them. Yeong-dae felt relaxed since it was his day off.

"Yeong-ran, let's never lose each other again," he said, locking eyes with his sister. "There's no one left but the two of us now."

"Sure, Yeong-dae. Let's not lose each other. Now, if we can just get Meiyang . . ."

Yeong-ran's voice trembled and abruptly stopped, and tears welled up in her eyes.

"Meiyang?" Yeong-dae asked with a vague sense of foreboding. "Who's Meiyang?"

"Never mind. It's nothing. Come on, Yeong-dae. Hurry up and eat your food," she said.

Yeong-ran quickly changed the topic as she handed him some chopsticks.

"Yeong-dae," she said when they finished eating, "why don't you go back to the restaurant for now. I have to work in the afternoon anyway. We can see each other whenever we want now. Let's meet this evening and talk some more."

Yeong-dae could tell that Yeong-ran was worried about what her boss might think. He headed back to the barbecue restaurant, planning to return that evening. He felt like he was walking on air.

Yeong-ran's Secret

As he waited in his room for the beauty parlor to close for the day, Yeong-dae got extremely bored. Cheol-i had gone out some time earlier, bragging about his girlfriend, and he hadn't gotten back yet. Yeong-dae stuffed the crumbled bills he was saving in his pocket and hurried outside, not bothering to put his cap on. He decided to buy a present for his sister. He followed Xita Street for a while and then turned into an alley lined with shops selling fashion accessories and costume jewelry. As he thought about what to buy for his sister, he realized that this would be his first time ever to buy a present.

In North Korea, Yeong-dae remembered, people usually gave food as gifts, but he had no idea what he ought to get here in

Shenyang. But even so, he wanted to buy Yeong-ran something.

So far, Yeong-dae had saved up all the money he'd made at the barbecue restaurant, and he still had the money that Mr. Park had given him as well. Yeong-dae continued walking around the accessory stores, but he couldn't think of what would be good to buy. He toyed with the idea of getting his sister a hairpin, but then it occurred to him that Yeong-ran lived and worked in a hair salon and probably had plenty of those. He paused for a second in front of a lingerie shop but was too bashful to go inside. The necklaces and brooches in the next store looked pretty, but he was too timid to ask how much they cost. As he tried to decide on a gift, he remembered the notebook that Yeong-ran had given him. He wished it hadn't been taken from him.

Yeong-dae passed the time walking around the same group of shops. Eventually, he gave up on the idea of buying clothing or jewelry and went to a street stall to buy some dumplings instead. It was the first time he'd paid for something in Shenyang. As he handed over the money and reached for the bag of dumplings, he noticed two police officers walking in his direction. Yeong-dae snatched the bag and started running toward the closest alley. When the officers saw him, they took off after him. Yeong-dae was running flat out, down one alley and then turning into another. One of the police officers blew his whistle, and Yeong-dae threw the bag of dumplings to the side and picked up the pace. The officers were right on his tail.

I'd rather die than let them catch me, just when I found my sister! They can't catch me. I won't let them catch me.

Yeong-dae gritted his teeth and kept running. He turned into another alley and ran until he came to a dead end. There was nowhere he could go. Just then, a door in the building next to him opened, and an old woman came out, pulling a wheelbarrow behind her. The wheelbarrow was loaded with a couple of big bundles. Yeong-dae put his hands together as if to pray, hoping she'd understand that he was in trouble. Then he jumped into the wheelbarrow and buried himself beneath the bundles. The old woman stared at Yeong-dae goggle-eyed and was about to say something when she heard the footsteps of the approaching police officers. Yeong-dae held his breath.

The boy's fate was out of his hands now. The officers asked the old woman something in Chinese. Yeong-dae's heart skipped a beat. She answered them in a level voice. Next, he heard the officers running off again. Before long, everything was quiet again.

The old woman tapped Yeong-dae's head where it was hidden beneath the bundles in the wheelbarrow. He cautiously lifted his head and looked around. No one was there but the old woman.

Yeong-dae finally released the breath he'd been holding. The old woman grinned at Yeong-dae. She must have pretended that she hadn't seen him. Yeong-dae bowed low several times to show her how thankful he was and then scurried out of the alley.

He regretted how rash he'd been at the market. The prospect of seeing his sister had made him so giddy that he hadn't even bothered to wear his cap before going out. That had been his mistake. People said the Chinese police could spot a defector at a single glance. The two officers had obviously seen something suspicious about Yeong-dae.

Yeong-dae made his way to Fushun Street, moving cautiously but quickly. He was frustrated about losing the dumplings he'd gotten for Yeong-ran. It hadn't been easy to work up the courage to buy them, and then he'd dropped them while running from the police. The big bag of dumplings would've been a feast for *kkotjebi* in North Korea. Yeong-dae thought about buying some more for his sister, but he was worried that the police might find him again. Instead, he decided to head straight for the beauty parlor.

When he got there, all of the hairdressers had gone home, and only Yeong-ran was left waiting for him. Since he'd barely escaped the police, he felt very nervous.

"What's wrong, Yeong-dae?" Yeong-ran asked when she saw how upset he looked. "Did something happen to you?"

Yeong-ran could tell something was the matter just by looking at her brother's face. He told her how he'd bought her some dumplings but lost them while the police were chasing him. They were the first present he'd ever bought for her, and he felt so upset about throwing them away. Taking his hand in hers, Yeong-ran brought her brother into the little closet.

"It's OK, Yeong-dae. We can pretend that I ate them. I'm just relieved that you didn't get arrested. How long do you think we'll have to keep living like this?"

The story about the chase made his sister upset. Yeong-dae wished he hadn't told her about it.

"I guess you didn't have any dinner either, did you?"

Yeong-dae shook his head in response. Yeong-ran reached over and picked up a small, square package that was lying in the corner of the room.

"Have you ever had ramen noodles, Yeong-dae? This is called Shin Ramyun. It's from South Korea."

Yeong-ran handed him the package. The plastic wrapping said "Shin Ramyun" in Korean and had Chinese characters on it that he couldn't read. Yeong-ran boiled some water in a pot and put the ramen noodles into the water. Next, she took a small bag out of the wrapping and sprinkled some powder from it into the pot. A fragrant aroma began to fill the room. Before long, it was all done, and the two of them started to eat. It was much better than the noodle dishes Yeong-dae had had in North Korea.

"Yeong-ran, isn't this kind of expensive? If they made it in South Korea, how did it get here?"

Yeong-ran answered him with a smile.

"There are lots of South Koreans here and all sorts of South Korean products as well. South Korean ramen is a little pricey, but I buy it sometimes because it tastes so good. Go on and dig in!"

When Yeong-ran spoke about South Korea, there was pride in her voice.

Yeong-dae had thought all his troubles would be over when he found his sister, but he still felt anxious after his run-in with the police.

"Yeong-ran, what do we do now? Do we have to keep living in hiding like this?"

His sister slowly shook her head.

"No, we can't keep living like this. Now it's our turn to experience a life without fear."

When he heard this, Yeong-dae sat up straight.

"How do we do that?"

Yeong-ran looked Yeong-dae in the eye for some time without speaking.

"What is it, Yeong-ran?"

Finally, she let out a long sigh and spoke.

"Yeong-dae, there's something I need to confess to you."

Yeong-dae's heart leapt into his throat. What did his sister need to tell him? He waited for her to keep talking with baited breath.

"When I left home," she said, "I walked straight into the trap that those bad people had set. After we crossed the river, they blindfolded me and put me in a car. There were four women from the Republic, including me. We were riding in a compact van. One person was driving and another was keeping an eye on us. I'm not sure how long we were in the van, but my whole body felt sick, I felt nauseated, and I even threw up.

"We finally arrived in a town called Helong. There, they drove us to a house in the middle of nowhere and tied us up. That's when we finally realized that something had gone terribly wrong. No matter how much we cried and begged, it was no use. We were there for several days, and during that time, they only fed us just enough to keep us alive. I couldn't tell you how much we begged them to tell us where they were taking us and to take us back home. At some point, my throat went hoarse, and I couldn't speak anymore.

"On the third day, some Chinese people we'd never seen before came to take us away. All four of us were split up and taken to different places. I saw money changing hands. We were being sold. I was taken to the house of an older unmarried man who ran a duck farm. He was living there with his elderly mother. The man . . ."

Yeong-ran's voice suddenly broke off, and she started to sob.

Yeong-dae's eyes narrowed when he heard his sister mention a duck farm.

"Did you say a duck farm in Helong? The duck farm with the crazy owner?"

Yeong-ran raised her tear-stained face and looked at her

brother with surprise.

"That's the one, but how did you know that?"

Yeong-dae had a sinking feeling in his stomach. He was thinking about the story he'd heard from Mr. Choe, the Joseonjok man who had taken him and Nam-sik in when they crossed the river. Mr. Choe had told him about a duck farm in Helong, and that was the same duck farm his sister was talking about. So his sister was the North Korean defector who had run away from that farm! The man running the duck farm was mentally disturbed, and he'd had a baby with the defector. Could that be the "Meiyang" his sister had mentioned that morning?

Yeong-dae couldn't believe it. He'd gone all the way to Wangqing County looking for her, and his sister had actually been sold to a duck farm in Helong.

Everything seemed to fit, but Yeong-dae was reluctant to admit that it was true. He wanted to believe that the duck farm his sister was talking about wasn't the duck farm he'd heard about. He just couldn't tell his sister that he'd heard about it before. He didn't want to dredge up painful memories.

"Oh, I don't remember. Anyway, Yeong-ran, what happened next?"

After a long pause, she began talking again.

"Yeong-dae, I did a bad thing."

Yeong-dae was taken aback. He wasn't sure what his sister was trying to say.

"When I ran away from the farm, I left behind my own daughter," Yeong-ran went on, with tears in her eyes. "I have to find her. I have to find my poor baby girl. The day the police arrested me, I'd gone to get her. The police took me back to the Republic. They put me through all kinds of awful torture, but I endured it all by thinking about my daughter Meiyang and begging her for forgiveness. Yeong-dae, I'm so ashamed to be telling you all this."

She wiped her eyes again. Yeong-dae thought his heart was going to tear right in two.

"Ashamed? There's nothing to be ashamed of, Yeong-ran. Anyhow, this Meiyang you're talking about, she must be my niece. All right, I'm going to help you. I'll bring back Meiyang, and then the three of us can go to South Korea. If we go there, I hear that they'll give us money and a place to live. Cheer up, Yeong-ran! I'm going to go get Meiyang."

He felt like some kind of mysterious energy was flowing through his body. His heart ached when he thought of what his sister had gone through, and he wanted to do something to help her. But his words just made Yeong-ran cry even harder.

"I'm sorry about this, Yeong-dae. If we leave Meiyang there, she won't have anyone to give her a good upbringing. Her father is crazy, and her grandmother is too old to raise her. That's why we have to go get her. Yeong-dae, can you forgive me? I'm so sorry."

Yeong-ran was sobbing even louder.

"Yeong-ran, I'm happy to have a new family member. You did the right thing. Before, it was just you and me, but now I have a niece. Why shouldn't I be happy? Don't cry, Yeong-ran. You've got to stop crying so we can make plans for getting Meiyang out of there. That's enough crying. I should ask Mr. Park for help."

If it hadn't been for Mr. Park, Yeong-dae couldn't have found his sister. He'd have to thank the missionary before asking him for another favor. But if he told Mr. Park about his situation, he was sure the man would do what he could. Yeong-dae pulled out the piece of paper with Mr. Park's phone number on it and dialed the number. That paper was one of his most prized possessions.

"Hello? Mr. Park, this is Yeong-dae. Do you remember me?"

On the other end of the phone, there was a pause.

"You know, Yeong-dae Lee! The boy you met in the cave. I'm in Shenyang now."

At that moment, Mr. Park must have remembered who Yeong-dae was, because he began to speak in an excited tone.

"Oh, sure! Of course I remember you. It's been quite a while. So, did you find your sister?"

When Mr. Park heard that Yeong-dae was in fact with his sister that very moment, he congratulated the boy. He sounded as pleased as if it had been his own sister.

"It just so happens that I'll be going to Shenyang in four or five days," the missionary said. "Are you still at the same barbecue restaurant?"

Yeong-dae felt as happy as if he were going to meet a relative he hadn't seen in years.

"Yes, I sure am, and I'm doing quite well, thanks to you! I guess I'll see you in a few days."

For some reason, Yeong-dae thought that everything would work out OK. But what made him the happiest was the thought of doing something to help his sister.

Yeong-dae was well aware that rescuing Meiyang from the duck farm wouldn't be easy. Even so, he still thought that everything would look different after Mr. Park got there. His sister told him that she'd been saving up money little by little so that they could go to South Korea. Yeong-dae wanted to use the money that he'd been saving to help rescue his niece.

Meiyang's Little Hand

Mr. Park had said he'd be coming in four or five days, but five days passed and he still hadn't come. Yeong-dae was getting worried since Mr. Park didn't pick up the phone when he called him. Had he gotten caught along with the defectors he was helping? When Yeong-dae remembered how Mr. Park said he was always in danger, he felt even more anxious.

A week after their phone call, Mr. Park finally showed up at the barbecue restaurant to see Yeong-dae. At last, the boy was able to relax a little.

"Did the family I was traveling with make it safely to South Korea?" Yeong-dae asked.

"They managed to leave Chinese territory, though it took

them longer than we planned. They're probably in some other country, though. No doubt they'll be in South Korea soon enough."

Mr. Park told him about their journey. On the way to the border, they had switched buses in the middle of the night to keep the police off their trail. After taking the family as far as the border, Mr. Park had returned to Shenyang by way of Beijing.

Yeong-dae quickly wrapped up his work at the restaurant and then headed to the beauty parlor with Mr. Park. His sister had finished cleaning up and was waiting for him. As soon as she saw Mr. Park, she thanked him for helping Yeong-dae. After that, she pleaded with him to help her rescue Meiyang. He tilted his head to the side and hesitated before answering.

"I'm not sure if we can bring her here without permission from Meiyang's father or grandmother. If something goes wrong, they could report us, too, and then we'd all be in big trouble. There are quite a few children in situations like that. It's really heartbreaking, isn't it?"

Yeong-dae had pinned all of his hopes on Mr. Park, and now he was at a loss for what to do. He wanted to go to Helong and sneak Meiyang out of the duck farm, but he was afraid of getting caught by the police and taken back to North Korea. If he was arrested again, he knew he'd face even worse punishment than last time. Since Yeong-dae had been helped by a South Korean missionary, he might be locked away in a concentration camp for political prisoners—or even put in front of a firing squad.

Mr. Park told them that children like Meiyang whose mothers were North Koreans sold in China were not given any identification papers. This meant that they couldn't even go to school. It was hard enough for defectors like Yeong-dae and Yeong-ran to live in hiding in a foreign country. But Meiyang couldn't get papers even though she'd been born in China. It was illegal for Chinese men to marry kidnapped North Korean women, and any children they had were not even treated as people.

When Yeong-ran heard what Mr. Park had to say, she started to cry.

"There's only one thing we can do," he continued. "If we offer Meiyang's father or grandmother some money, they might let us take the girl. If they aren't able to take good care of her anyway, saying the right things and giving them some money might persuade them to give her to us.

"But the most important thing is for them to hear us out. If they aren't willing to listen, there's little we can do. The easiest way is for Yeong-ran to go herself and plead with the family. She's the child's mother, after all. But that option is risky. If she says the wrong thing, they could call the police."

Thinking of her daughter made Yeong-ran want to drop everything and go to her right away, but when she thought about the duck farmer, she started trembling uncontrollably.

"This isn't a normal man we're talking about," Yeong-ran managed to say. "If I show up, there's no telling what he might do. I lived like an animal there."

Yeong-dae couldn't bear to watch his sister cry like that. He asked Mr. Park if there was anything he could do.

"Why can't I go instead? I want to go and rescue Meiyang."

Mr. Park firmly shook his head in response to Yeong-dae's question.

"That would be even more dangerous. Let's take some time and figure this out. There has to be some way to do this."

Yeong-ran abruptly lifted her head.

"One way or another, I have to rescue Meiyang. I can't leave my child there. I should have never left her there. I have to get her out of there so I can raise her and give her a good future."

Watching his sister sob, Yeong-dae felt so bad for her.

"Yeong-ran," he said, "it's not your fault. You're a good person. You shouldn't blame yourself like this. I mean it, Yeong-ran."

Yeong-dae felt like he was about to cry, too. Mr. Park spoke to them quietly.

"I know a missionary named Susannah. She's a Joseonjok woman. Susannah works to help children who have no nationality like Meiyang get adopted. If I talk to Susannah about your situation, we'll probably come up with something. Just give me some time."

When Yeong-ran heard this, she stopped crying. Yeong-dae felt a little better as well. The rest of that evening and into the early morning, Mr. Park was on the phone calling various people. As he finally got up to go, he turned to Yeong-dae and his sister.

"I have to go to Yanji now. Sometime tomorrow or the next day, Susannah will visit you. You'll want to talk this over with her. I'll help in any way I can, too."

Yeong-ran reached into her purse and pulled out some money.

"Please take this, Mr. Park. If you're going to work, you'll need some money."

But Mr. Park waved the money away.

"I don't need the money. Talk it over with Susannah, and if she needs any money, you can give it to her. Rest assured, she's someone you can trust."

Without taking the money, Mr. Park departed immediately for Yanji. He said some North Korean defectors who had crossed the river were hiding there, waiting for him. Yeong-dae was reminded of the days he spent in the cave.

Mr. Park said Susannah would arrive in a day or two, but she came to see Yeong-ran after five days. Susannah began by asking a lot of questions, such as what Meiyang's situation was and whether the duck farmer was worth talking to or not. After Yeong-ran told her the whole story, she shook her head and frowned. If they weren't careful, Susannah said, they could find themselves in an awkward situation. Susannah offered to go to Helong disguised as a peddler and find out exactly what was going on with Meiyang. Yeong-ran gave Susannah some money for her trip.

For Yeong-dae, each day that passed after Susannah left for Helong felt as long as a year. His sister didn't eat much of anything and seemed to be half out of her mind. Yeong-dae was so worried about his sister that he slept at the beauty parlor at night and went back to the barbecue restaurant early in the morning to work. Even while Yeong-ran was sleeping, she called Meiyang's name in her sleep. Five days passed, but Susannah still didn't return. Yeong-dae started getting even more worried about his sister.

A week after she left, Susannah returned from Helong. As soon as Yeong-ran saw her, she started bombarding her with questions.

"So how was she? Is my darling Meiyang doing all right? Was she feeling OK?"

Susannah waited until Yeong-ran was finished and then began speaking.

"Meiyang is doing OK. She's in good health, but they say she has trouble speaking. Meiyang's father isn't the sort of person you can talk to. I did talk to the grandmother, and she seems sincere in her concern for Meiyang. Not only is her son not in his right mind, but she herself is old and weak. She seemed to feel bad that she couldn't take good care of Meiyang. She said Meiyang always carries around an old pillow full of millet hulls. Her grandmother said Meiyang's mother made the pillow for her . . ."

When Yeong-ran heard this, she burst into tears again.

"Ah, that pillow! Meiyang, Meiyang . . ."

Yeong-ran couldn't finish the sentence, so Susannah went on.

"Most of the children of North Korean women sold in China don't have any identification papers. Meiyang doesn't either. Her father and grandmother are hard up for money, too. They can't afford to pay the large sum necessary to buy fake papers for her.

"Yeong-ran, if you told them you wanted to take the girl, they might decide to make things difficult. Meiyang's grandmother seems to hold a grudge against you. I asked the woman what she thought about giving up Meiyang for adoption overseas so that she can grow up in a better environment. At first, she threw a fit. But after she calmed down, she said she was getting older and didn't know how much longer she had. She said she'd think about it."

"She wasn't suspicious of you?" Yeong-ran asked.

"I told her that I know people who help children get adopted. I told her not to tell her son about this no matter what and to call me if she changed her mind. I don't think it would be good for you to talk to that woman, Yeong-ran."

This made Yeong-dae think that they might be able to rescue

Meiyang after all.

"The living conditions there are terrible," Susannah went on. "Meiyang's father has stopped working on the duck farm, and her grandmother is getting older and says she's in poor health. When I said we could give them some money, she looked tempted. Let's wait a little longer."

They waited for a few more days after Susannah left. Yeong-dae was afraid they wouldn't have enough money to get Meiyang, so he gave all of his money to his sister. Once again, Yeong-ran apologized to Yeong-dae for taking his money as tears welled up in her eyes.

"Yeong-ran, don't be sorry. You're all I have. Why would I treat you like a stranger? We're the only two people left in our family. It makes me happy to think about getting Meiyang and living together. Yeong-ran, I don't want to hear you say you're sorry anymore. What's yours is mine, and what's mine is yours."

It was hard for Yeong-dae to believe that he was already 16 years old. He wanted to be someone his sister could trust and depend on. He couldn't wait to bring Meiyang to Shenyang. He thought that his sister wouldn't be sad anymore when his niece finally got there.

A few days later, Susannah came to see them again. She told them that Meiyang's grandmother had promised to give Meiyang to Susannah in five days. Yeong-ran was so excited that she could barely eat, and Yeong-dae was thrilled at the thought of seeing Meiyang, too.

Four days later, when Susannah was about to leave for Helong, she was barely able to keep Yeong-ran from going with her.

"You need to stay right here, Yeong-ran," the missionary said. "You can see Meiyang tomorrow. If you rush things, you never know what kind of trouble you might bring on yourself. Rest assured. I will bring Meiyang to you."

Yeong-ran gave Susannah some money and begged her to bring back Meiyang quickly and safely. Yeong-dae couldn't concentrate on work that day and felt even more nervous the next. He couldn't believe how slowly time seemed to pass. As he worked, he kept looking at the clock on the wall. By the time the restaurant closed that evening, Yeong-dae was itching to go and could barely sit still. Once he was done working, he ran straight to the beauty parlor.

Thinking that Meiyang was already there, he bought some bread and snacks on his way. When he opened the door of the hair salon and went inside, his heart was pounding furiously.

"Yeong-ran, is she here? Is Meiyang here?"

But the beauty parlor was too quiet. He opened the door to his sister's room. Susannah and his sister were sitting on the floor with mournful expressions on their faces.

"Where's Meiyang? What happened to Meiyang?"

Yeong-dae pressed Susannah to answer him.

"Susannah wasn't able to bring my daughter back yet," Yeong-ran said instead. Her eyes were red and puffy.

Yeong-dae's heart dropped into his stomach. Susannah explained what had happened in a calm and measured voice. Meiyang's grandmother had promised to give the girl to her, but when Susannah showed up, she suddenly demanded a huge amount of money.

Yeong-dae asked, "How much . . . how much did she ask for?"

Yeong-ran answered him in a voice drained of energy.

"More than all the money I've managed to save so far."

"Even including the money I gave you?"

She nodded sadly. Susannah told them that there was no other option. Yeong-ran explained the situation to the owner of the beauty parlor and borrowed some money from her, and

Yeong-dae persuaded Mrs. Kang at the barbecue restaurant to lend him some, too. He believed with all his heart that family was more important than money. Whatever it took, they had to get Meiyang back. They could always make more money.

A few days later, they came up with the money they needed.

As Susannah was about to leave for Helong, Yeong-ran said the same thing to her over and over again.

"You've got to bring us Meiyang, Susannah. Bring her back safely, please."

"I will. But instead of worrying, you should be thinking about what you're going to do when your little girl gets here. Why don't you cook something tasty for her?"

Susannah patted Yeong-ran's hands to comfort her. After seeing Susannah off, Yeong-dae went back to the barbecue restaurant. He was supposed to go to the bus terminal that evening with his sister to pick up Meiyang, and he grew more impatient as he waited. As he was scrubbing the wire grills, he seemed to hear the second hand of a clock ticking away inside him. Sometimes, he'd realize that he'd been wiping the same spot on the grill for several minutes in a row.

Yeong-dae was so restless that Mrs. Kang called him over when the lunch hour was over.

"Today's the day your niece is coming, isn't it? Why don't you go spend this time with your sister? I'll have someone else do your work in the kitchen."

"Are you serious, Mrs. Kang?" Yeong-dae asked. "Is it really OK to go?"

"You bet. Go on, now!"

Yeong-dae was so thankful that he gave his boss an extra low bow. He ran to his room and changed clothes. This time, he remembered to put on his cap, pulling the brim down low. Then he was off, racing toward the beauty parlor where his sister worked.

When he got to the beauty parlor, his sister was even more agitated than he was. She absentmindedly picked up the clothes she'd bought for Meiyang and then set them down again. She played with the hairpin she was going to put up Meiyang's hair with, putting it in her own hair and looking in the mirror.

Yeong-ran kept glancing at the clock.

"Yeong-dae, I think the clock is losing time. It must be broken."

"No, it's showing the right time. I got here right after lunch."

"No, time just can't be going this slow. I really think

something's wrong with it."

While Yeong-ran was glaring at the clock and muttering to herself, the owner of the beauty parlor spoke up.

"The clock is fine, honey," she said. "You're just impatient because you want to see your daughter. You're planning to go to the bus terminal, right? Why don't you head over there right now instead of waiting around impatiently here? What time is her bus supposed to arrive anyway?"

"She's supposed to be getting here around six in the evening."

The director clucked her tongue in sympathy.

"You've still got time to kill. Even if you head over there an hour from now, you'll still have plenty of time."

Yeong-ran must not have completely trusted the salon owner because she kept glancing at the clock. Yeong-dae was itching to go, too, and he tried taking a deep breath. But that didn't help him calm down.

"Yeong-ran, why don't we just go the terminal and wait there? I can't bear sitting still like this."

"OK, Yeong-dae," she said. "I feel the same way. Let's get going."

Yeong-dae and his sister went to the bus terminal together. It was still two hours before the bus from Helong would arrive.

When Yeong-dae saw his sister pacing around nervously, he suggested that they sit in the waiting area. But Yeong-ran was too fidgety to stay in her seat for long.

"Yeong-dae," she told her brother, "I want to take Meiyang and go somewhere where we'll be treated like people."

His sister's eyes were wet with tears.

"Sure, Yeong-ran," he said, choking up. "We'll do that, and Meiyang will be there with us."

The bus arrived right on schedule. As soon as they saw the bus, Yeong-dae and his sister ran toward it. Susannah stepped off the bus, holding a little child by the hand. Meiyang was clutching a dirty little pillow. It was the pillow her mother had made for her.

"Meiyang!"

Yeong-ran took Meiyang in her arms and held her so tightly, touching the pillow. The little girl looked uncomfortable and her mouth twitched, as if she were about to cry. She'd been so young when her mother ran away that she didn't seem to recognize that Yeong-ran was her mother. Yeong-ran sobbed as she gazed at her daughter's face.

"Meiyang, it's me, your mom! I'm sorry. I'm so sorry."

The little girl seemed confused about what to do, and she

gave no response. Yeong-ran was still hugging her tightly. She wasn't willing to let go of her.

"Meiyang, I'm your uncle!" Yeong-dae said. "We're going to live together, and you won't be separated from your mother again. I promise!"

Yeong-dae held out his hand to her. Meiyang hesitated and then finally held her hand out to him. Yeong-dae took the little hand and held it tightly. He could feel the warmth of his niece's body flow into his.

Epilogue

On Children's Day[1], Yeong-dae, Yeong-ran, and Meiyang took a trip to Seoul Land. Yeong-ran had gotten up early that morning to make some *kimbap*, rolls of rice wrapped in dried seaweed, for their lunch. Schools were closed for the holiday, and the amusement park was bustling with families. Around the park, they could hear children's gleeful screams bursting into the blue sky of May like a fountain and then dying down again. Meiyang pointed excitedly at a popular attraction called the Viking ship that swung back and forth like a pendulum. Full of screaming passengers, the big ship dived down, slicing through the air like a whale.

"Wow! That looks like a lot of fun!" Meiyang said. "I want to ride that one, Yeong-dae."

"You want to go for a ride on the Viking ship? Isn't that a little scary?" Yeong-dae said.

---

1. Children's Day is a public holiday in South Korea that falls on May 5th.

"No, it's not! It's not scary at all. I rode the Gyro Drop[2] too, you know!"

Meiyang hopped up and down, begging Yeong-dae to let her ride the Viking ship. There were no longer any traces of pain or shyness in her face.

"Well, Meiyang, I guess you're even braver than me! All right, you can go on the ride. Can you do it by yourself?"

"I want you and Mom to ride it with me!"

At this, Yeong-ran waved her hands, pretending to be afraid.

"Me? I can't go! It's way too scary!"

"Mom, there's nothing scary about it! Don't worry—I'll hold you tight!" Meiyang said in a grown-up voice, throwing her arms around her mother's waist.

The three of them got in line to ride the Viking ship. There were so many people in line that Yeong-dae guessed it would be a while before their turn came.

As Yeong-dae looked at the children around them, he was reminded of his little sister Yeong-ok. Children's Day was celebrated in North Korea, too, but things were different there. Most kids took part in mock drills and battles, competing

---

2. The Gyro Drop is a popular ride at Lotte World, an amusement park located in Seoul.

for prizes. Yeong-dae couldn't remember ever spending the holiday with Yeong-ok. Thinking of Yeong-ok made him want to do everything he could for Meiyang. His sister Yeong-ran was worried he would spoil her, but Yeong-dae wanted to give Meiyang the love he had been unable to give Yeong-ok.

Two years after rescuing Meiyang, Yeong-dae and his sister arrived with her in South Korea. Now, three years had passed since they completed the training program for defectors at the Hanawon Resettlement Center and moved into a government-subsidized apartment.

During that time, Yeong-dae had completed a middle school program at an alternative school, and he was now in his first year of high school. Most South Koreans his age had already graduated high school, but he hadn't been able to study when he was a *kkotjebi*. Once he reached South Korea, he'd had to catch up on his elementary and middle school coursework.

Meiyang, on the other hand, had been in South Korea since kindergarten and was now in the second grade of elementary school. She had a lot of friends and was thriving at school.

In his dreams, Yeong-dae sometimes relived his experiences as a *kkotjebi* and his escape from North Korea. The dreams were so vivid that when he woke up his entire body would be drenched in cold sweat.

With the help of the missionary Mr. Park, Yeong-dae, his family, and other defectors made the 3,000 km journey from Shenyang to the southern border of China. They crossed into another country and then trudged through a thick jungle on their way to yet another border. After stopping at a refugee camp in Bangkok, they finally reached South Korea. On their long journey, they had crossed international borders no less than four times.

Not all of the defectors made it to South Korea, though. Some were arrested by the police and sent back to North Korea, while others succumbed to sickness and injury. Yeong-dae's family had been pretty lucky, actually. He was not religious, but he thought that they couldn't have completed their journey without some help from above.

Immediately after graduating from the program at Hanawon, Yeong-ran got a job at a beauty parlor. At first, she worked as an assistant, but she had recently made the leap to full hairdresser. Each month, she donated a little of the money she earned to a charity helping stateless children living in China. There were tens of thousands of children in China whose mothers were North Korean defectors—children just like

Meiyang. Each time Yeong-ran thought of those children, she hugged her daughter tightly and breathed a sigh of relief.

Yeong-dae had also decided he would help the *kkotjebi* when he was done with school. He hoped that would help him get over the guilt he still felt about Yeong-ok. He wanted so badly for the word "*kkotjebi*" to vanish from the face of the earth. He longed for the day when North Korean children would be able to study and play like other children. Yeong-dae's dream was that children in North Korea would not have to suffer what he had suffered as a *kkotjebi*.

"What's on your mind, Yeong-dae? It's our turn!"

Yeong-dae snapped out of his daydream to find Meiyang tugging on his hand. It was time to board the Viking ship.

"OK! Let's get on!" he said.

Yeong-dae and Yeong-ran sat down with Meiyang between them and fastened their seat belts. The Viking ship slowly moved forward, going up into the sky. Just when Yeong-dae felt the blood rushing to his head, the ship suddenly went into reverse and plunged down, throwing Yeong-dae's upper body forward. Meiyang squealed, and Yeong-dae and Yeong-ran both screamed at the top of their lungs. It occurred to Yeong-dae that this was the first time he had ever screamed so loud from sheer pleasure. He couldn't remember the last time Yeong-ran and Meiyang had laughed like this, either.

The sky is blue,

and my heart is glad.

Let the accordion play! . . .

We have nothing to envy in the world.

Yeong-dae wasn't sure why this North Korean song suddenly popped into his head, but he felt like he finally understood the true meaning of "nothing to envy."

Still moving backward, the Viking ship swung up in the air again, defying gravity. Yeong-dae found himself crying. Maybe it was because he had been laughing and shouting so much, or maybe it was because he felt so good. Yeong-ran gestured at him, asking what was wrong. Yeong-dae shook his head to say that he was fine.

As the Viking ship switched directions and swung down once more, the buildings of the amusement park far below came racing up toward them. Yeong-dae, his sister, and his niece screamed as the ship reached the bottom of the swing and then soared up into the sky. *No, nothing is wrong, Yeong-ran. What could be wrong?* Looking at his sister, he shook his head and smiled. *Yeong-ran, I'm never going to cry again!*